SPILLY JANE MITTENS

SPILLYJANE KNITS

COOPERATIVE PRESS
CLEVELAND, OHIO

SPILLY JANE MITTENS

ISBN 13 (PRINT): 978-1-937513-68-9

FIRST EDITION

Published by Cooperative Press
http://www.cooperativepress.com

FOR COOPERATIVE PRESS

Senior Editor: Shannon Okey
Art Director and Assistant Editor: Elizabeth Green Musselman
Book Designer: Kim Saar Richardson
Technical Editor: Andi Smith
Additional layout work by Lise Anderson

FOR MY FLOCK

CONTENTS

FOREWORD

I may be SpillyJane's biggest fan. Her work combines invention with precision, and creative energy with discipline in a way that I find quite unique among today's hand-knit designers. No one is able to take the small canvas of a mitten and use it to suggest a moment in time; celebrate the structure of ordinary objects; or neatly capture the essence of a thing quite like SpillyJane. In her mind, Victorian architecture and tasty snacks exuberantly co-exist, and the range of reference in her work is often startling.

You'll be surprised and delighted as you turn the pages of this book: one design features a bunch of sneaky gnomes, while the next is a thoughtful evocation of the aesthetics of fossilized coral. Some of these mittens will blow your mind with the deft way in which they manage complex ideas and narratives (Decadence); others will please your eye with their elegant simplicity (Midtown).

Smart and witty, bold and handsome, I also feel that that Spilly's designs have important implications in the way that they suggest how pattern plays a role in the structure of of the everyday. After absorbing yourself in this book you may find yourself, like her, observing meadows and pavements and imagining them on a mitten.

And as well as a baker's dozen of beautiful patterns, inside you'll find a straightforward and inclusive introduction to mitten-making to entice even the most uncertain beginner.

If you love making mittens, this tome is an essential addition to your bookshelf. And if you have never knit a pair, the following pages will show you how. So pour yourself a cup of tea, sit down with yarn and needles, and enter the marvellous, mitten-filled world of SpillyJane.

—Kate Davies

PREFACE

When I first (re-)learned to knit and began to really take it seriously about nine years ago, I thought that I'd be making plain scarves and socks forever. Not that there is anything wrong with either of those options, but when I happened upon the colourful Latvian mitten tradition something changed. I instantly fell in love with the colour, pattern and symbolism that the Latvians lavished upon what could otherwise be a simple functional accessory for keeping one's hands warm. Here was a tradition that transformed a functional garment into something extraordinary. Not only were the resulting objects beautiful, but also the sense of history and the length of this knitting tradition just blew me away. I picked up Lizbeth Upitis' wonderful, bilingual LATVIAN MITTENS, and I've been in love ever since.

I wanted to start knitting colourwork mittens right away. My skills, however, were lacking, as I had never knit anything in colourwork before. Once I had completed a few colourwork projects and felt I had a handle on the skill set, I just had to take these patterns and symbols and see what I could come up with myself—so I sat down and made up my first mitten, Sea Mineral Mittens. Later that week I was walking past the ornate ironwork gates of a local park and I thought they would look nice on a pair of mittens. They did, and that pattern became Willistead. Nearly simultaneously, I kept thinking how great a simple motif—maybe a fish?—would look repeated over and over again in different coloured stripes on mittens, this became Swedish Fish. And that's how it all happened.

Fast forward a handful of years and a whole pile of SpillyJane Knits patterns, and here we are today with you holding this book in your hands. I hope you like it.

With fondness,
JANE (SPILLY)
Windsor, ON
October 2015

INTRODUCTION

WHY MITTENS?

I am very passionate about mittens, probably more than most people. Mittens are wonderful things; not only do they keep your hands warm, but they provide an approachable—and eminently porta-ble!—knitted canvas on which colour and pattern can be combined to create meaning, and an attractive garment.

When you make mittens you are participating in a tradition that has been around for as long as peo-ple with thriving knitwear cultures have had fingers that could get cold. This is especially true when one works with ancient colour palettes and patterns, but equally valid when one is working mittens with a more contemporary pattern or theme. You are still working the ancient garment shapes and with the same intent as ancient people around the world—to keep your fingers, or the fingers of someone you know—warm.

Mittens are unique in that they are functional accessories, special little garments that are hap-pily able to be as fancy or as plain or as odd in decoration as one likes. You might get weird looks for having tiny gnomes or fish or cupcakes all over a larger garment, but relegate these designs to your hands and suddenly you're an individual with consummate taste. That little pop of colour and pattern about the hands is the perfect touch to the minimalist winter outerwear ensemble.

A note on the multiple sizes

In this book most of the patterns are offered in up to three different sizes. Please take a moment to read through your selected pattern in its entirety, highlighting the correct numbers where applicable

in order to ensure that you are actually making the mitten that you want to produce.

MITTENS AND FINGERLESS MITTENS

Thumbs

When knitting mittens there are several different options for thumbs. As such, almost every pattern in this book offers two different thumb options. These are two of the most popular styles: the Peasant Thumb (also known the Afterthought Thumb) and the Gusset Thumb (also known as the Sore Thumb.) Some knitters favour one over the other; some may work both with no preference. Both possess their own sets of pros and cons, as is discussed below. You may wish to try just one style of thumb or both, as both methods develop skills that are well-worth adding to your knitter's bag of tricks.

Most of the samples in this book feature the Peasant Thumb, though the option for switching them to Gusset Thumbs is also presented below (page 23).

THE PEASANT THUMB

By construction, the Peasant Thumb is basically a small knitted tube that is picked up and worked from the completed body of the mitten.

Some knitters love this thumb because it means that you can just work the mitten as a tube, not having to worry about anything other than the colour-work pattern, which is especially convenient when working a complex stranded design. When off the hand and lying on a surface the mittens' thumbs are discreetly tucked away and you are left with an elegant pair of pointy-tipped, intricately decorated colourwork tubes, their splendor unmarred by any extraneous appendages.

You may choose to work the thumb so that it matches the pattern on the palm of the mitten. But if you find that after working the rest of the mitten you are tired of the pattern, you may opt for a simple colourwork pattern like checks or stripes, or even a solid colour. There is nothing wrong with choosing the simple, single-colourway option—in fact all of the patterns in this book go that exact route.

Some knitters, however, don't care for the Peasant Thumb. They don't like how it just sprouts out of the palm; the way it distorts slightly while worn on the hand. Some say that they find it somewhat uncomfortable while worn. The best way to decide your own preference is to try working a pair of mittens with Peasant thumbs for yourself. Give the Plain Blue Mitts with Peasant Thumb on (page 30) a try; make one or make both so you can practice this technique without having to commit to a full pair of mittens.

THE GUSSET THUMB

The gusset thumb differs mainly from the peasant thumb in that it is formed through the use of a gusset—that is, a triangular piece of fabric that protrudes from the body of the mitten to accommodate the broader base of the thumb. The gusset is created simultaneously while working the body of the mitten until it is big enough to enclose the base of the thumb.

The resulting mitten possesses more of a natural hand-shape and therefore allows for a more natural-fitting mitten. Some knitters prefer this as it feels more comfortable on the hand and there is less distortion present in the resulting fabric when the mitten is worn.

Some knitters just don't like the way that the Gusset Thumb juts out from the body of the mitten. Some, however, fancy it as a charming and classic shape that is not to be trifled with (just ask any knitter from Michigan!). Regardless, the mirrored increases used in creating a Gusset Thumb are handy techniques to pick up; it never hurts to get your head around a different style of increase. If you'd like to give the Gusset Thumb technique a try without committing to making an entire pair of mittens please see the Plain Brown Mitts with Gusset Thumb pattern below on page 40.

CONVERTING TO GUSSET THUMBS

Most of the patterns in this book are written with the Peasant Thumb. If, however, you decide you prefer the Gusset Thumb, conversion is a relatively simple process. When converting the patterns in this book that have peasant thumbs to gusset thumbs, the gusset will always be "grown" on the second last stitch of the chosen round. It is recommended that the gusset should begin at least two inches below the point where the recipient's thumb protrudes from the palm. You may find that you prefer your gusset to start a few rounds higher or lower than this, which is perfectly fine. If this is the case simply knit a few more or fewer rounds before you begin working the gusset. The stitch where the gusset begins (second last on your chosen round) will remain the same.

WORKING WITH YOUR NEW GUSSET

When working a Gusset Thumb on a colourwork mitten it is important to ensure that both colours in use are properly distributed and carried across the gusset being created. Colourwork Gusset Thumbs can be one of the most attractive and exciting bits of a stranded mitten. Working the Gusset Thumb in a very simple colourwork pattern makes it easier to keep track of your increases and makes the whole process more enjoyable and relatively painless.

In this book, as the gusset is merely an option, I have not designed specific gusset motifs to match each pattern; instead I have included a few simple ways below that you might choose to decorate your gusset. I have also included a blank thumb gusset chart on which you can add a design of your choosing (see appendix).

Here are just some of the ways you can decorate your gusset:

Plain thumb If you choose to work the thumb plain carry the second colour behind the first colour wrapping it behind your stitches as you work.

Stripes Stripes are a simple and decorative motif and are a nice counterpoint to any of the mitten patterns included in this book. They're also a handy way to keep track of your progress as you work your gusset.

Lice Stich Yes, the name is rather odd, and rather old, but this is my preferred method for working thumb gussets. It serves to carry both colours across the gusset so that they are ready to go at the beginning of the next needle. It has the added benefit of being extremely decorative.

FINISHING YOUR GUSSET THUMB

You can finish the tip of the Gusset Thumb in the same manner as the Peasant Thumb. You can also use the thumb from the Under The Hostas Mittens pattern on page 68 as well as in the appendix on page 136. This thumb finishing method features spiral-type decreases at the tip. This allows for a more rounded finish to the thumb tip, which may be preferred in a mitten with a thumb gusset.

REQUIRED SKILLS

Before you start knitting you should be familiar with the following techniques:

Knitting in the round
Knitting with double-pointed needles
Increases/Decreases
Long-tail cast on
Stranded colourwork techniques
Knowledge of basic mitten construction
Picking up stitches
Kitchener Stitch

If you are unfamiliar with any of these techniques, ample resources can be found online including tutorials and videos.

A NOTE ON FIBRE CHOICES

The patterns in this book have been designed and worked in 100% wool yarns.

I am something of a wool enthusiast; I can't get enough of the stuff. The attributes of wool are practically endless—it's a wonderful insulator, it holds its shape and actually gets warmer as it takes on moisture, which makes it perfect for mittens.

Wool is a wonderful fibre to use for colourwork. Its hairy, scaly fibres give it "grab" that allows the different yarns to hang on to each other as you work. If you've ever worked with really slick, slippery yarns, you will immediately see this benefit of wool. The other benefit in using wool for colourwork is that when worn, the strands on the inside of the mitten will felt and provide you with a garment that is twice as thick and warm. Any yarn that contains at least 70% wool will behave in this way. Please note that super wash wool—wool that has been processed so that it will not felt under normal conditions—will not.

I understand that some people have an aversion to wool, or even wool allergies, so please feel free to use other fibres (animal, plant or otherwise) in your work if that is your preference. Just be aware that the mittens that you end up producing will not behave in the same way as the ones made of wool shown here.

A NOTE ON CIRCULAR KNITTING

The patterns in this book are written to be worked on one set of five double-point needles. This traditional method is my preference, but if you prefer to knit in the round using two circular needles or the Magic Loop method, stitch counts per needle will be different. The charts lend themselves quite easily to conversion.

MITTEN FIT

Do not be alarmed if the mittens you produce don't fit snugly. As written, most of the patterns in this book are meant to produce mittens that are a little larger than the hands that will eventually end up wearing them. When working a full pair of mittens, a slightly larger mitten is always better than a slightly smaller one. A larger mitten will fit better and also keep you warmer because it allows a warm air pocket to form between your hand and the knitted fabric.

That said, sometimes you might prefer a slightly tighter fitting mitten, particularly when making fingerless mittens. Over time a tighter-fitting fingerless

mitten worked from wool will stretch and become a bit looser.

YARN WEIGHT

The mitten patterns in this book are designed and written for fingering weight yarn. To properly execute the mittens you must use fingering weight yarn or the mittens won't end up being the correct size. If you were to substitute DK weight yarn in any of these patterns the resulting mittens would be gigantic. Save yourself the time and heartache and stick with the recommended fingering-weight yarn.

GAUGE

Gauge is important in any form of knitting if you want to produce usable, wearable garments and accessories. Please take the time to ensure that the gauge you are getting matches the one prescribed by the pattern you are working from. You may find, depending on your own personal knitting style and tension, that you need to go up or down a needle size in order to get the proper gauge. If you do not get the recommended gauge your mittens will end up being smaller or larger than intended.

The patterns in this book call for thinner needles than you may be used to. As such their stitch counts are rather high per round. If you increase the size of the needle too drastically you may find that you are producing a hat rather than a mitten. Don't let this worry or scare you, just keep an eye on your work as you go and it will be fine.

A NOTE ON COLOURWORK AS "SCARY"

I have heard people talk about colourwork and charted knitting as "scary" about a million times. I promise you that it is not. When I was first starting out making colourwork things, yes, it did seem a little daunting but at no point was it actually scary. It's just the same old Stockinette stitch knitting that you're used to; you're just going to be working it with two balls of yarn. This is not a new, terrifying concept. People have been knitting like this for hundreds of years, and they all had to learn at some point. You can knit colourwork mittens and you can knit them well. If you don't know how to do this yet, you can learn. Trust me.

The patterns in this book generally employ two colours per round, and three colours <see pattern Under The Hostas, page 69>—only when absolutely necessary. Remember, sneaky duplicate stitch can be used after the mitten is finished to add wee bits of colour that would have been too much of a pain to add while the mitten was initially worked.

WORKING WITH CONTRASTING COLOUR

If you want to knit colourwork mittens like the ones in this book and knit them quickly, painlessly and well, this is the number one skill to develop.

The best way to keep your yarns sitting properly without having to constantly fret over them is hold them in two different hands. Take care to carry your new yarn (the Contrast Colour) up and over your old yarn (the Main Colour) in the same fashion every time you switch yarns to ensure that the stitches in your finished fabric are consistent. This can make the difference between a clearly patterned fabric that is pleasing to the eye and one that is confusing and muddled.

This will make your work go faster and prevent your yarns from becoming tangled while you work. Once you work an entire pair of colourwork mittens using this technique you will be a pro. Like riding a bicycle, it will become second nature.

Two-handed knitting requires the use of the English and Continental styles at the same time. Most knitters tend to use one or the other in non-colourwork knitting, but it is useful to know both. This is not nearly as difficult as it may sound. If you are less than confident in one or the other, a little practice will allow you to become proficient enough to use both at the same time. I always hold the background colour in my right hand and knit

it English style, and knit the motif Continental style with my left hand. Continental tends to produce a slightly looser stitch, which may be a bit larger than those knit English style. When you knit the motif in the slightly looser Continental style the stitches sit slightly differently in the resulting fabric. Your colourwork motif will stand out better than it would if both were knit in the same style.

My one caveat is that once you start knitting in this way you must take care to remember which yarn was held in which hand and be careful not to switch hands mid-mitten. The colourwork knitting you work with your right hand will look significantly different from that worked with your left. Maybe this won't bother you one sausage—or maybe it will. Chances are no one will notice or even care, but now is the chance to stick to good knitting habits before the bad ones sneak in through the door behind them. Do whatever you like, but consistency is key.

A NOTE ON LEFTOVER YARN

Whether you knit a few or just one of the patterns in this book you're going to end up with half-used skeins, or nearly-complete skeins that you've just taken a wee nibble out of. That's the nature of colourwork!

But there's another side to this issue as well. You will need to acquire various colours and shades of yarn. As you do this, stick to two or three basic, sturdy yarn lines. You're essentially building up a palette—a stash—of colourwork yarns that you'll be able to draw from in the future. If you buy a skein for one pattern, you might end up with enough yarn for another pattern in the future.

But that's not all you can do with those odd half-used bits of yarn—you can also use them to produce stripey fingerless mittens like the Plain Blue and Brown Mitts on <pages xx and xx>, respectively.

YARDAGE

When working colourwork mittens please allow 1.5 yards / 1.37 m per colour per round. Do not forget to double this number as you will be making a pair of mittens. This suggested yardage is an approximation only, and is probably an overestimation. It is better to have over-estimated your yarn requirements rather than to find out all too late that you don't have enough.

MITTEN LENGTH

The patterns in this book are offered in up to three different sizes, both width- and length-wise. When it comes to length you may find that you need to lengthen or shorten the mittens accordingly, in which case simply knit a few more (or fewer) rounds before you begin decreasing for the fingers. The measurement that you will be dealing with here is that from the crook of the thumb to the tips of the fingers. A good rule to follow is to work past the Thumb Placement (when working with the Peasant Thumb) or the completion of the Thumb Gusset (once it's been placed on waste yarn) to the tip of your index finger before decreasing for the fingers. You may wish to take this measurement ahead of time and then measure the piece as you go or you

could simply try the mitten on as it's being worked to be sure it's the right length. If you're ever in doubt, remember that a longer mitten will always fit better than a shorter one, which will simply be too small and won't fit properly. If you're worried about it, err on the side of caution and knit a few more rounds, just in case.

DEALING WITH ENDS

It's a sad, but true, fact: when you do colourwork you are going to end up with ends. Two of the pesky things per colour used, every time. Even with a two-colour mitten you're going to end up with at least four, and that's not counting the ends produced from working the thumb! Sooner or later you are going to want to weave those ends in, so you might as well get used to the idea.

The best way to do this is to flip the mitten inside out and to weave your ends in and around on the wrong side of your work. I usually opt for a sort of duplicate stitch technique where I weave the ends in following the reverse Stockinette pattern on the inside of the mitten for about an inch or two—just to make sure that they're not going to go anywhere. Sometimes, especially with intricate patterns, it can be difficult to see the reverse Stockinette on the inside due to the stranding produced by the colourwork pattern. Just gently weave the ends in and around the stranded floats until they are secure—the general rule is to do this for an inch or two.

Do not break your yarn after every round! Carry those colours for as long as you can, because a break in your yarn means extra ends—one for where you break the yarn and one for where you have to rejoin it to start working with it again.

Sometimes you might find that you've broken a working yarn too soon. There are a couple of ways to deal with this: you could always leave another tail and simply rejoin the yarn where it is needed, but this will end up giving you a few more ends to have to deal with. If you are using wool you can perform what is rather unappetizingly called a "spit splice" to rejoin the working yarn to the tail you just dropped. Simply take up the end of the tail of yarn and gently pull the plies apart and fluff up the fibres for about an inch. Do the same with the end of the working yarn. Lay the two fluffed-up ends on top of each other so that they overlap. Moisten the ends of the yarns and roll them together between your palms briskly until they felt into a single strand of yarn. Continue working with this yarn as needed.

If you're only dealing with a couple of ends here and there on your mitten (less than 10 or so ends— don't think you'll be able to do this with the Cupcake Mittens!) you can get away with not even bothering to sew those ends in. Yes, you heard me right! I have happily worn some of my own woolen colourwork mittens for several Winters now—mittens on which, for some reason or other, I never bothered (or never got around to) sewing in all the ends. And in all honesty they were perfectly fine! I couldn't feel the ends when I was wearing them, and stitches directly attached to the ends didn't budge. The thing about colourwork mittens is that, when worked in wool the heat and the moisture from your hands combine with friction to felt the floats in place on the inside. The same thing goes for these ends. They won't go anywhere!

A sneaky trick to secure ends without having to sew them all in is to leave long ends so you can braid them together later. Flip the mitten inside-out and gently brush all the ends so that they lay away from the body of the mitten. Gather ends that are nearby each other into small groups of about six or so, and divide these into threes and then braid them for an inch or two. Tie the braids off with a small knot and trim the ends of the tails neatly. Then just tuck the wee braids into the inside of the mitten and you're all set—you won't even notice them when you wear the finished mitten.

DESIGNER TIP

The above sneaky trick is a brilliant tip and best put to use when working the Cupcake Mittens (see page 84) as all the colour changes can result in many, many unruly ends that will need to be dealt with!

FINISHING YOUR MITTENS

You might find that when you're working your mittens your colourwork might appear slightly puckery—the fabric won't sit perfectly flat and it might pull in a little bit around the areas where you switched yarns. This is perfectly normal in pre-blocked colourwork and it is nothing that a slight press and steam can't fix. Even if your mitten looks perfectly fine before it is blocked you will find that a quick steam pressing with an iron (set to the "wool" setting, of course,) can work wonders in evening out stitches and unifying the overall quality of the design on the piece.

A NOTE ON THE BLANK CHARTS IN THE APPENDIX

You've seen some of my mittens; why not try your hand at producing a pattern of your own? In the appendix you'll find a series of blank charts in multiple gauges and sizes to help you do just that.

Ideas for new mitten patterns can come from anywhere. Don't settle for plain old mittens! Maybe you have a store-bought pair of favourite socks that have worn out and aren't worth saving. Try translating their pattern into knitted stitches and turning them into mittens. Then you can enjoy them for longer, in a different way. If you have seen a pattern in a stitch dictionary that you'd like to try on a sweater but just aren't ready for that kind of commitment, you can try it out on a mitten first. See if you like it as a knitted fabric before you spend all that money on yarn and tie up all those needles for so potentially long. The best part is you will get a pair of your own original colourwork mittens out of the deal.

Happy knitting and have fun!

PEASANT THUMB

Work the body of the mitten until there is enough fabric to cover the wearer's wrist (as per pattern or as desired) and the heel of the hand up to where the thumb protrudes from the palm. This round is referred to as "the Thumb Round." Work across the Thumb Round as per pattern until the needle where the thumb is going to be placed is reached. Knit the correct number of stitches on this needle up to where the thumb stitches are set to begin.

Drop both working yarns. Take up the piece of waste yarn (a 15"/38 cm length of yarn in a comparable weight and a highly-contrasting colourway) and begin to work the appointed number of thumb stitches (as dictated by pattern).

You will end up with a small strip of stockinette stitches worked in the waste yarn that is equal to the width of the thumb, like this.

Slip all the stitches that you just worked in the waste yarn back onto your left-hand needle and get ready to work them again—this time in pattern with your working yarn(s).

Just pretend that the waste yarn isn't there and go on working your mitten as per its pattern.

Work to the end of your waste yarn stitches so that the waste yarn is completely encased by pattern stitches. Draw the ends of the waste yarn down inside the completed body of the mitten as you work. Give the ends a tug (if needed) to make sure they're in no danger of unravelling out of the mitten on their own.

Continue working the mitten in pattern to the fingertips and finish the tip as per your pattern. You'll end up with a mitten that looks like this.

Now that the mitten body is complete it's time to pick up around those waste stitches and begin working the tube that will act as your Peasant Thumb. Prepare to pick up stitches for the thumb. You will be picking up these stitches from the body of the mitten directly below the stitches that you worked in the waste yarn.

Holding the mitten right-side up (with the cuff at the bottom and the fingertips at the top) and without removing the waste yarn, slip the tip of a double-pointed needle under the left-hand "leg" of all the stitches directly below the stitches you worked in the waste yarn. Be careful not to split the yarn as you pick these stitches up.

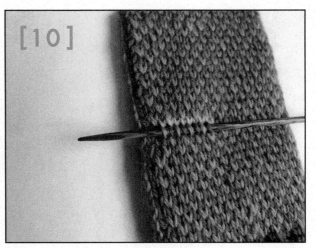

Continue picking up stitches in this manner until you have a number of stitches equal to the number that you worked in the waste yarn on your needle.

Now, flip the mitten upside down so that the fingertips are on the bottom and the cuff is at the top. Begin picking up stitches across the TOP (from this angle, the bottom, but STILL the top) of the stitches ABOVE (below) the waste yarn stitches. Keep in mind that these stitches will be upside down.

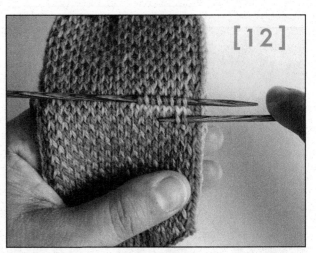

Slide the tip of your double-pointed needle beneath the right-hand "leg" of these stitches (actually the left-hand "leg", but right-hand here since you're working upside down), and continue to pick up stitches equal to that which you picked up below (as well as being equal to the number of stitches you originally worked in the waste yarn).

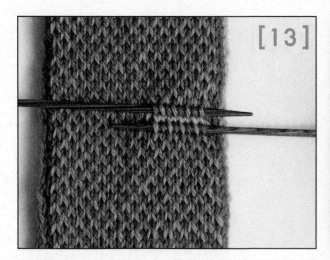

You will end up with an equal number of stitches across two opposing double-pointed needles and a configuration that looks something like this.

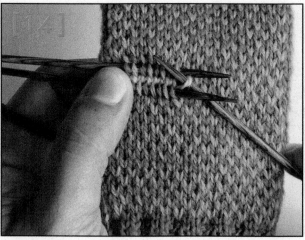

Now it's time to start removing the waste yarn. Flip the mitten back around so that the cuff is at the bottom and the fingertips are at the top. Carefully slip a third double-pointed needle beneath the first "leg" of the first stitch worked in waste yarn and use the needle to gently pull it away from the body of the mitten.

Continue to carefully—and gently—remove the waste yarn one leg at a time, detaching it from the stitches of the body of the mitten that you had previously worked around it. If you picked up the stitches around the waste yarn properly you are in no danger of losing them. Take care to ensure that they are securely positioned in the centre of your holding needles and not in any danger of falling off.

Here is the mitten with all the waste yarn stitches removed. The stitches that you picked up along the top (the proper top) of the thumbhole might look a little strange, especially if they are worked in colourwork. This is normal. Just try to keep them in the proper order for now. Once the first round of the thumb has been worked they will return to normal. Begin picking up extra stitches and working the actual thumb.

[17]

When working the thumb you will be picking up two stitches in each of the "corners" for a total of four picked-up stitches. These stitches both help to close up the inevitable holes at the corners of the thumbs as well as allow for extra movement. Pick up your first stitch before you begin to work the thumb stitches on what will now be known as Needle 1. Pull this needle (Needle 1) away from the body of the mitten, exposing the strands between the stitches there and the stitches on the needle. Choose which of these strands you wish to pick up—in pattern if possible. Here we'll be picking up the green strand since the first stitch on Needle 1 is purple and we'll be staying in pattern.

[19]

You can place this new stitch the right way round on Needle 1 if you prefer; in this case be sure to knit this stitch through the back of the loop so that it results in a tighter, twisted stitch.

[18]

Slip the tip of your double-pointed needle beneath the chosen (here, green,) strand and place it backwards on Needle 1 in front of the to-be-worked stitches. Place it backwards on Needle 1 so that you won't forget to work it as a twisted stitch. You'll be working this stitch as a twisted stitch in order to tighten up the corner of your thumb.

[20]

Continue working all the stitches across the front of the thumb with your chosen yarn (or as per pattern.) Divide these stitches in half across two double-pointed needles to make it easier to work in the round. These Needles will now be known as Needle 1 and Needle 2 respectively.

When you have worked all the stitches across the front of the thumb it is time to pick up the second of the four "corner" stitches. Once again, pull the needle you were working with away from the body of the mitten, just as you did in Step 17 above. Choose a strand as per the pattern (or as per your whim) and lift it up with the tip of your working needle and place it appropriately (in the same manner as you did in either Step 18 or Step 19,) on the end of Needle 2. Work this new stitch as a twisted stitch to tighten up the corner of your thumb.

Before you begin working the stitches on Needle 3, pick up another stitch in the corner once more just as you did in Step 17. Take care to knit this stitch through the back as well. Work all stitches across the back of the thumb, working them as twisted stitches (through the back of the loop) should they require tightening (which they probably will.) These just-picked-up stitches across the back of the thumb are notorious for looking strange at first, just knit them twisted for now so that the back of your thumb has a solid grip on the body of the mitten. They will behave as normal stitches from here on in and once the rest of the thumb has been worked you will hardly notice them wgen the mitten is finished. When all these back-of-thumb stitches have been worked pick up one final "corner" stitch and place it on the end of Needle 3 (again, as per Step 17.) Work this stitch as a twisted stitch as well.

The first Round of the thumb is now complete, and your mitten should currently look something like this. Tuck the tail of your working yarn down through the thumbhole so that it stays out of your way as you continue to work the thumb to the desired length. Complete thumb as per pattern.

Work the body of the stranded, colourwork mitten until the round dictated by the pattern where the thumb gusset is set to begin. Work around this round until you arrive at the "seam stitch." Before you work this stitch pull the needles apart so that the strands between the "seam stitch" and the previous stitch are exposed. Choose the strand that is the same colour as your seam stitch—in this case it is the Contrast Colour (CC), the darker shade of green. Begin the first of the thumb gusset increases—the Make 1 Left (MIL).

Slip the tip of your working needle beneath this strand and place it on your needle front-to-back.

The MIL increase is now complete. The resulting stitch should look like this.

Using the same dark green yarn (the CC) knit this stitch through the back of the loop to twist it.

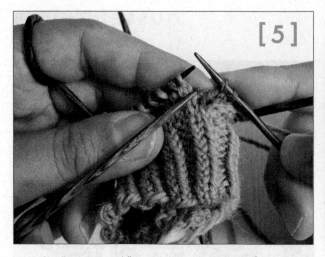

Knit the "seam stitch" with the CC yarn. Before you work this stitch pull the needles apart so that the strands are visible between the "seam stitch" and the next stitch to be worked. Locate the CC strand between the two stitches. Begin working the increase that is mirror image of the M1L increase that you just worked—the Make 1 Right (M1R).

CARRYING YARN OVER EXTENDED DISTANCES

Some colourwork patterns—especially non-traditional ones—will require the use of one colour more frequently than the others. You may even find that you end up with lengthy stretches (six stitches or more) over which you must carry the yarn you are not using. If you worry that the wearer's fingers might get caught in these excessively long floats, you can prevent them by wrapping the yarn you are not using around the working yarn. Here's how to do it.

Here we have a mitten-in-progress where the Contrast Colour (CC), the yarn on the left, has been used for the past seven stitches. The Main Colour (MC), the yarn on the right, remains unused since the last needle. To further complicate matters, the MC is not going to be needed again for several stitches more, which means that it needs to be wrapped in behind the working yarn so that the inevitable extra-long float can be avoided.

 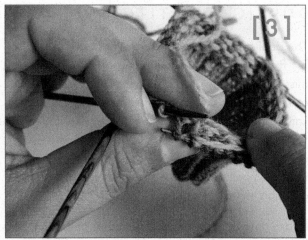

The first thing to do is to draw the yarn you are not using (here, the CC), over the working yarn (here, the MC). Drop the yarn you are not using and let it hang loose in front of the working yarn up against the back of the work. Leave the yarn you are not using there while you work the next stitch with the working yarn.

Here's the yarn you are not using firmly secured by working that next stitch with the working yarn. You may wish to check the front of your fabric to make sure that the yarn you are not using isn't showing behind the stitches that you used to tack it on. If it is showing through to the front, adjust the finished stitches with the tip of your knitting needle to lessen this effect.

When you're tacking an unused yarn to the back of your work in this way be careful to leave enough slack. If you don't you will end up with a distorted fabric with pulled and oddly-sitting stitches. You may find that certain patterns require you to skip an inordinately high number of stitches to achieve the desired design, which may mean that you'll find yourself performing this wrapping action several times over. Just make sure that you keep the carried yarn loose enough to accommodate the resulting fabric. When the time comes to work with that formerly unused yarn, take care to keep it slack enough to allow for the stitches you'll be working with it to sit nicely in the finished fabric.

DUPLICATE STITCH

The duplicate stitch technique is especially useful for fixing mistakes in colourwork patterns, such as a missed stitch or two, without having to rip back and re-knit. It allows you to alter previously completed knitted fabric using surface embroidery that mimics the look of stockinette stitch. In addition to the correction of mistakes, duplicate stitch can be used to add embellishment to a finished item, or to make a design element stand out.

Please note this technique should only be used for the correction of small mistakes; in some cases you may have to rip back and work the whole mitten over again. The duplicate stitch technique is, however, essential for the retention of your sanity and the general happiness of those who live with you.

FIXING MISTAKES

One of the most frustrating experiences when knitting complex patterns is to notice a mistake only after you have knitted for several inches past it. Few knitters, myself included, are content to live with mistakes in their colourwork knitting.

Some knitters recommend ripping all the way back to the offending stitches and reworking the entire piece, but that would mean the loss of many hours of work. Sometimes it is possible to correct the error with a few well-placed duplicate stitches in the same colourway. If done carefully and correctly, even you will have a hard time spotting the rectified stitches.

See the tutorials on the next two pages for help with both!

Here we have a mitten with a simple colourwork pattern that is sporting a few mistakes. This is nothing to worry about as these mistakes can be corrected using duplicate stitch.

Using a blunt tapestry needle threaded with a sufficiently long piece of yarn in the correct colourway poke your needle up through the "legs" of the stitch below the one that you're going to be correcting with duplicate stitch. Gently pull the full length of your yarn through this stitch making sure that you leave a long enough tail on the inside of the mitten (about 4"/10 cmss) so that it can be sewn in to the inside of the mitten when you're finished.

Insert your tapestry needle behind both "legs" of the stitch above the one that you're working on and gently tug the working yarn until the first leg (in this case, the right leg) sits flatly and evenly on top of the same leg of the stitch you're fixing. It is better that this new half-stitch be looser rather than tighter as tight duplicate stitch will distort the knitted fabric and ruin the desired effect.

Complete the other "leg" of the new duplicate stich by poking your tapestry needle back in the same stitch that you originally poked it out of—the stitch below the one that you're correcting. Ensure that the needle is going into this stitch at the exact point that the first leg came out of so that this new stitch will look as natural as possible. Now, slowly and gently tug your working yarn until the second "leg" of the new stitch sits as evenly in the fabric as the first one you just worked. You may wish to place your finger on the loop of yarn as it grows smaller to ensure that you don't pull your yarn too tight as you pass your yarn to the inside of the mitten. If working only one stitch, just pass the working yarn to the inside and gently break the yarn being careful to leave a long enough tail (4"/10 cm) for weaving in later. If you're fixing another stitch that's not too far away on the same (or a nearby round) you may wish to poke your needle up through the "legs" of the stitch below that of the one you intend to fix just as you did with this one, so it's ready to go for the next one.

[5]

Here we have the completed duplicate stitch disguising the mistake and looking as if it was always part of the mitten. When working additional duplicate stitches with the same yarn please take care not to pull too hard on the working yarn as doing so will distort the previously worked duplicate stitches. If that should happen, simply remove the working yarn and begin again, working carefully, slowly and gently.

EMBELLISHMENT

Duplicate stitch can also be used to add additional embellishment or decoration. All you need is a blunt tapestry needle and additional lengths of yarn. This is useful when you only need a little bit of extra colour on a relatively small portion of your mitten, whether it is part of an overall design or the only design component in use. Duplicate stitch is much

easier than using three (or more) yarns at a time when initially working the piece.

[1]

Here we have a completed—but rather plain—body of a mitten. The thumb hasn't been worked yet but that's ok, as it isn't going to interfere with the process of adding duplicate stitch.

[2]

Using a contrasting colourway of yarn and the same duplicate stitch technique as described above, additional detail or design elements added as desired using the "grid" of the worked knitted fabric as your canvas. Keep your embroidery stitches loose and even with the worked knitting in a similar tension. Tug the yarn gently as you work your duplicate stitches and they'll look like they had always been there.

PLAIN BLUE MITTS
WITH PEASANT THUMB

THESE FINGERLESS MITTS ARE A GREAT PLACE TO START YOUR colourwork mitten-knitting journey. They're a great way to use up leftover bits of yarn and for practising peasant thumb construction. You can find the peasant thumb tutorial on page 17.

SIZES

Women's S (M, L); shown in size M

FINISHED MEASUREMENTS

Length 5.79 (6.5, 7.12)" / 14.7 (16.5, 18.1) cm

Palm Circumference 7.1 (8, 8.8)" / 18.03 (20.32, 22.35) cm

MATERIALS

Knit Picks Palette (100% wool; 231 yds / 211 m per 50g ball)

» [MC] Celestial; partial ball
» [CCA] Hare Heather; partial ball
» [CCB] Serrano; partial ball
» [CCD] Tidepool Heather; partial ball
» [CCE] Marble Heather; partial ball
» [CCF] Celadon Heather; partial ball

1 set US #1 / 2.25 mm double-point needles

Stitch marker (optional)
Waste yarn
Yarn needle

GAUGE

9 sts = 1" / 2.54 cm in stranded colourwork pattern

11.25 rnds = 1" / 2.54 cm in stranded colourwork pattern

PATTERN

Cuff

Using the MC, CO 64 (72, 80) sts using the Long-tail cast on, or any other stretchy cast on. Distribute sts evenly across 4 needles—16 (18, 20) sts on each. The needles will now be known as N1, 2, 3 and 4 respectively. Being careful not to twist sts, prepare to beg to work in the rnd working the cuff as follows:

Rnd 1: [K2tbl, p2], repeat across all sts.

Repeat rnd 1 for the next 7 (9, 11) rnds, for a total of 8 (10, 12) rnds of ribbing. Prepare to work body of mitten, working from either left-hand or right-hand mitt chart S, M or L.

Mitten Body

Work from the appropriate chart, following from right to left. Please

---

DESIGNER TIP

There are a couple rounds of colourwork here and there in this pattern just for interest and for a little bit of colourwork practice if you're new to the technique. Try knitting with two hands on those colourwork rounds if you like!

note that the chart shows every st in every rnd. Continue working from the chart until rnd 32 (38, 41), where there is a mark denoting thumb placement.

DESIGNER TIP

These mitts run a little larger and looser. If you prefer a more fitted, tighter mitt, please go down a needle size.

THUMB PLACEMENT

For LH mitten: Work across all sts on N1. Work the first 2 (3, 4) sts on N2. Using a 15"/38 cm piece of waste yarn, knit the next 11 (12, 13) sts on N2. Slip these sts back onto the LH needle and work the remaining sts on LH needle. Work across N2, 3 and 4 in pattern.

For RH mitten: Work across N1 and N2. Work the first 3 sts on N3. Using the 15"/38 cm piece of waste yarn, knit the next 11 (12, 13) sts on N3. Slip these sts back onto the LH needle and continue to work in pattern. Work the remaining sts on N3 - 16 (18, 20) sts remain on N3. Work across all sts on N4 in pattern.

Work to the end of rnd 57 (65, 72). Complete fingerless mittens as follows:

Rnds 1–5: Using MC only, work [k2tbl, p2] rib across all sts.

BO all sts loosely.

Fingerless Mitten Thumb

Depending on whether LH or RH mitt is being worked, the thumb will be worked in either CCA or CCB, respectively. Pick up 11 (12, 13) sts both above and below the sts held on the waste yarn, along with a total of 4 sts from either side of the thumb hole, for a total of 26 (28, 30) sts, discarding the waste yarn when finished.

Divide the sts thus:

» Small size: N1 - 6 sts, N2 - 7 sts, N3 - 6 sts, N4 - 7 sts

» Medium size: 7 sts on each of 4 needles

» Large size: N1 - 7 sts, N2 - 8 sts, N3 - 7 sts, N4 - 8 sts

Work the thumb starting from the outer lower corner and working across the front of the thumb.

Rnd 1: K across all sts.

Continue working Rnd 1 until thumb reaches just below the recipient's thumb joint (or desired length.) knitting to the end of N4.

Small and Large sizes only: Dec 1 st on N2 and 4 on the last rnd - 24 (28) sts

Begin to complete thumb as follows:

Rnds 1–4: [K2tbl, p2] repeat across all sts.

Bind off all sts loosely.

Finishing

Weave in ends. Place mitten beneath a damp tea towel and press with a hot iron set to the wool setting to steam block.

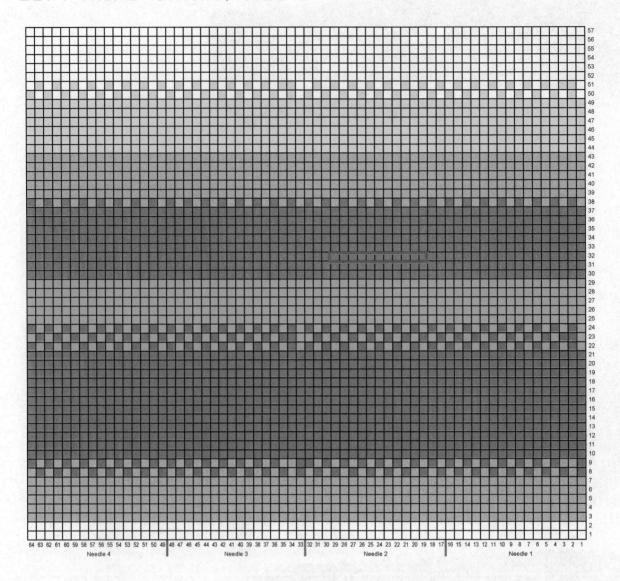

Needle 4   Needle 3   Needle 2   Needle 1

- ☐ Knit MC
- ▨ Knit Contrast Colour A
- ▨ Knit Contrast Colour B
- ▨ Knit Contrast Colour D
- ▨ Knit Contrast Colour E
- ▨ Knit Contrast Colour F
- ☐ Right thumb placement
- ☐ Left thumb placement
- ▨ No stitch

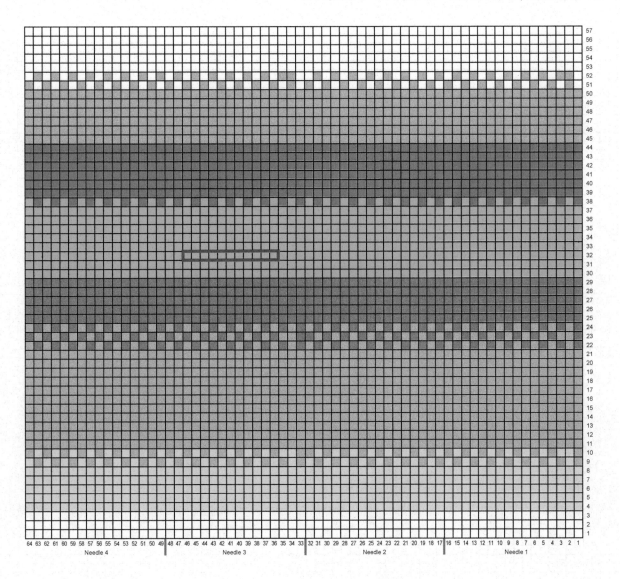

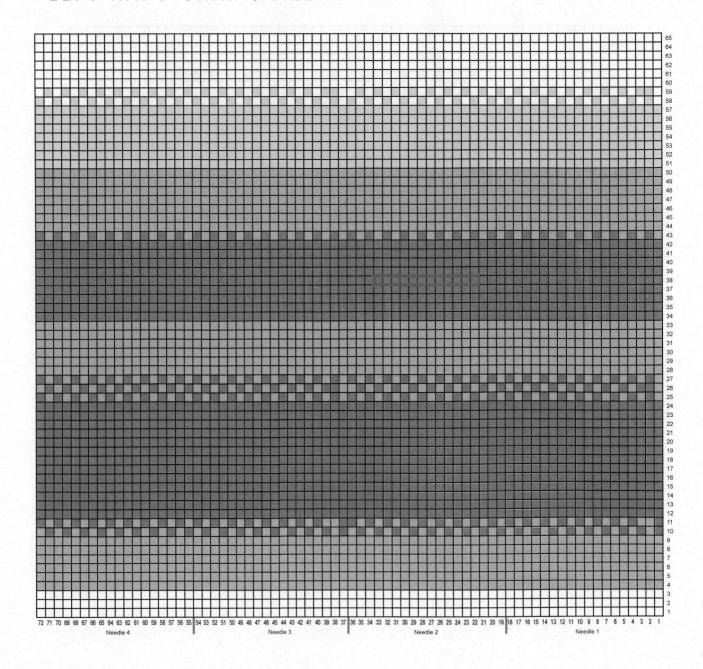

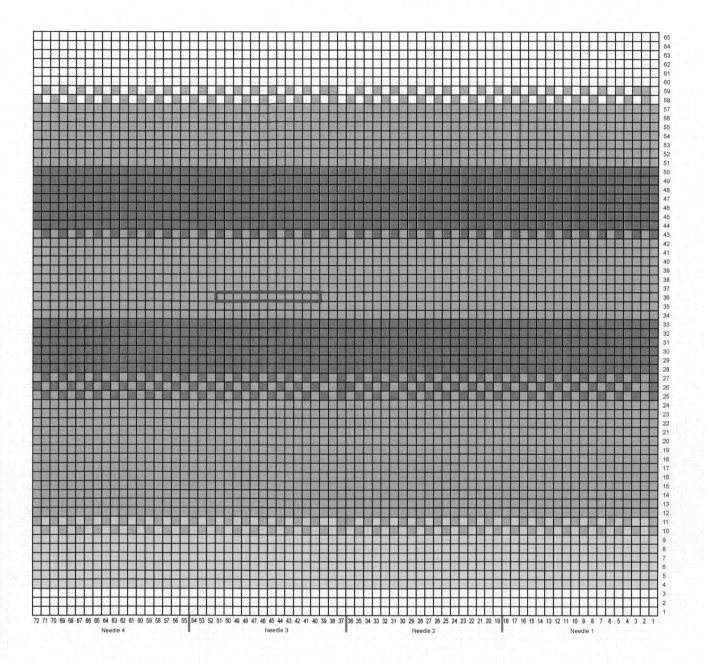

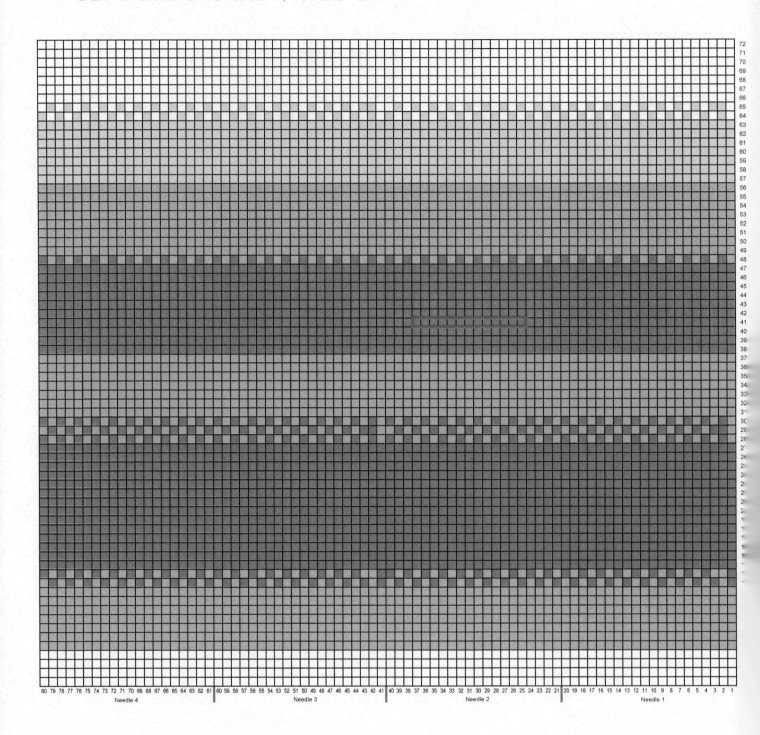

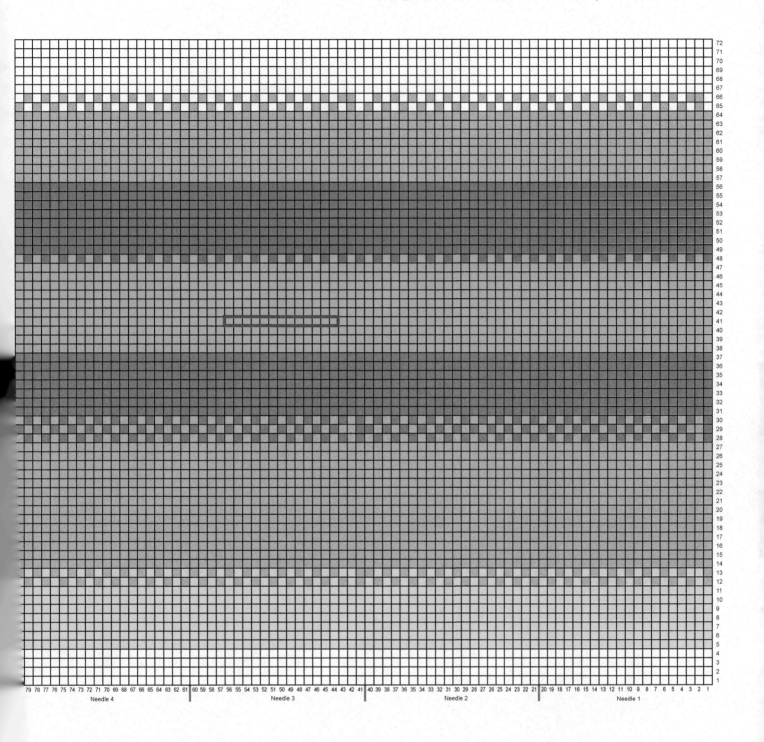

PLAIN BROWN MITTS
WITH GUSSET THUMB

THESE MITTS FEATURE TWO DIFFERENT CHARTS WITH RANDOM striping to give you options for your own personal pair of mittens. Knit two of one, two the other, or one of each; it's up to you. As the palm and backs of these mitts are identical it doesn't matter which hand you wear which on.

For an introduction to the gusset thumb see page x, for gusset thumb tutorial please see page 23.

SIZES

Women's S (M, L); shown in size M

FINISHED MEASUREMENTS

Length 5.58 (6.25, 7.08)" / 14.17 (15.9, 17.98) cm

Palm Circumference 6.58 (7.53, 8.47)" / 16.71 (19.12, 21.51) cm

To fit: 7 (8, 9)" / 17.78 (20.32, 22.86) cm, worn with approx. 0.5" / 1.27cm of negative ease

MATERIALS

Brooklyn Tweed LOFT (100% Targhee-Columbia wool; 275 yds / 251 m per 50g ball)

» [CCA] Pumpernickel; partial ball

» [CCD] Bird Book; partial ball

» [CCF] Hayloft; partial ball

Knit Picks Palette (100% wool; 231 yds / 211 m per 50g ball)

» [CCG] Thicket; partial ball

» [CCB] Finnley Heather; partial ball

» [CCE] Iris Heather; partial ball

1 set US # 1 / 2.25 mm double-point needles

2 stitch markers
Waste yarn or stitch holders
Yarn needle

GAUGE

9 sts = 1" / 2.54 cm in Stockinette stitch

12 rnds = 1" / 2.54 cm in Stockinette stitch

PATTERN

Cuff

Using the MC, CO 56 (64, 72) sts using the Long-tail cast on, or any other stretchy cast on.

DESIGNER TIP

These mitts as worked here are tighter-fitting for those who might prefer this sort of thing. If you'd like a looser fit, increase your needle size to US 2 / 2.75 mm.

Distribute sts evenly across 4 needles – 14 (16, 18) sts on each. The needles will now be known as N1, 2, 3 and 4 respectively. Being careful not to twist sts, work the cuff in the rnd as follows:

Rnd 1: [K2tbl, p2] repeat across all sts.

Rep Rnd 1 for the next 25 (29, 34) rnds, for a total of 26 (30, 35) rnds of ribbing, switching between CC yarns where denoted by the chosen chart.

Mitten Body

Work from chart S, M or L, following from right to left. Please note that the chart shows every st in every rnd. Continue working from your chart until Rnd 29 (33, 38) where there is a mark denoting thumb placement.

Thumb Gusset

Work your thumb chart in conjunction with your main chart until the end of Rnd 22 (26, 30) of thumb chart.

Next rnd: Begin working Rnd 61 (66, 76) of the main charts, and work up to the first st marker denoting the thumb gusset sts. Remove the first marker and transfer the 23 (25, 29) thumb gusset sts to a piece of waste yarn or small stitch holder and set them aside for the time being. Using the working yarn cast on

DESIGNER NOTE

The thumb chart details the increases required to work the thumb gusset of the mitt. Increases in the thumb gusset will begin on Rnd 3 of your chart and will continue on every other rnd until Rnd 22 (26, 30) - 23 (25, 29) sts, including one "borrowed" st from the body of your mitten.

Thumb chart placement is denoted on the main chart by the red rectangle, along with an asterisk on the rnd below, which represents the "borrowed" st.

Placing stitch markers on either side of this st when you first encounter it in Rnd 33 is recommended, as it will be easier to keep track of the thumb gusset's stitches this way.

1 st using the backwards loop method, directly after the live sts that have just been worked, which replaces the st that was "borrowed" earlier for the thumb gusset—there are now 56 (64, 72) sts in the body of the mitt again. Continue working the body of the mitt as per your main chart. The body of the mitt is now complete. Bind off all sts loosely, in pattern.

Thumb

Take 23 (25, 29) thumb gusset sts off waste yarn or holders and rearrange them as evenly as possible across 4 (or 3, if preferred) needles. Begin working in the rnd, following Rnd 23 (27, 31) of thumb chart. Work across all sts currently on the needles. Pick up and knit 1 (3, 3) sts from where the extra st

was cast on on the body of the mitt—24 (28, 32) thumb sts.

Continue working from thumb chart until the end of Rnd 31 (33, 37). The thumb is now complete. Bind off all sts loosely, in pattern.

Finishing

Weave in ends. Place mitten beneath a damp tea towel and press with a hot iron set to the wool setting to steam block.

■	MC	⚥	Ktbl	
□	Contrast colour A	⊙	Purl	
■	Contrast colour B	✳	Denotes gusset thumb placement	
▨	Contrast colour D	Ml	Left leaning increase	
□	Contrast colour E	MR	Right leaning increase	
□	Contrast colour F	M	Make 1	
■	No stitch			

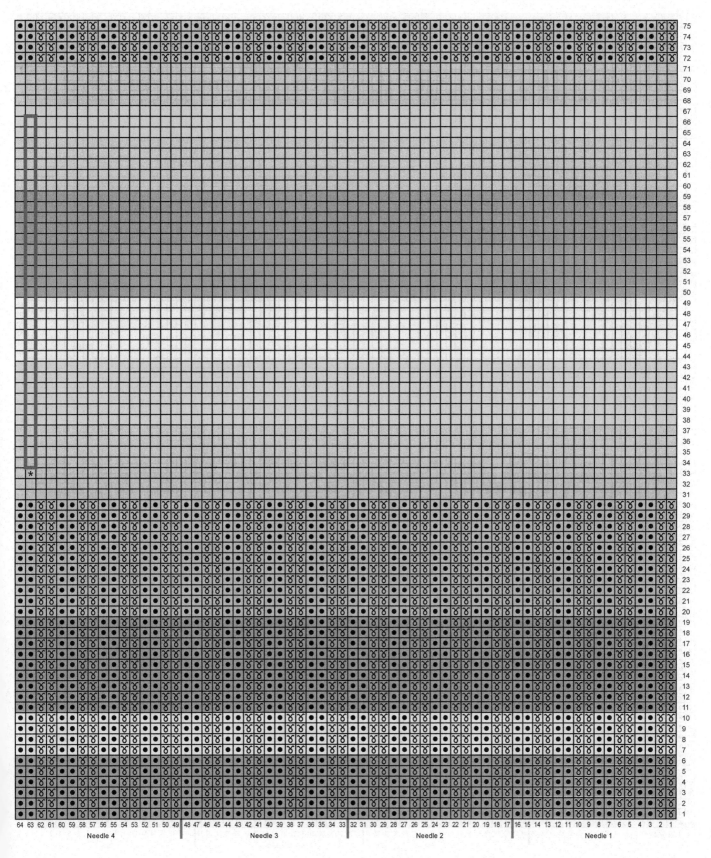

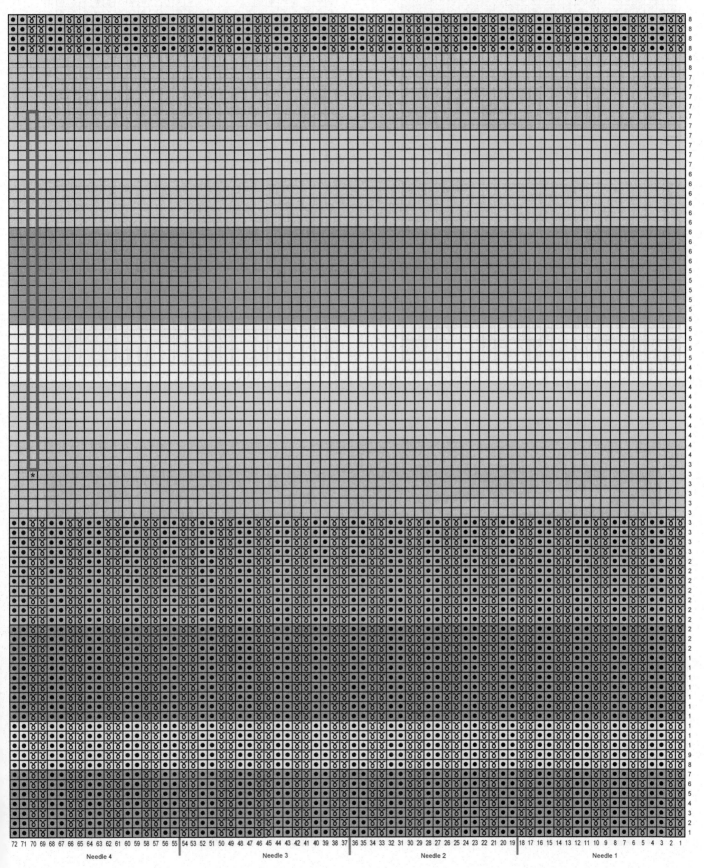

SMALL LEFT THUMB

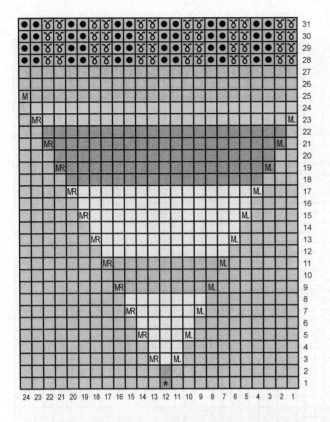

SMALL RIGHT THUMB

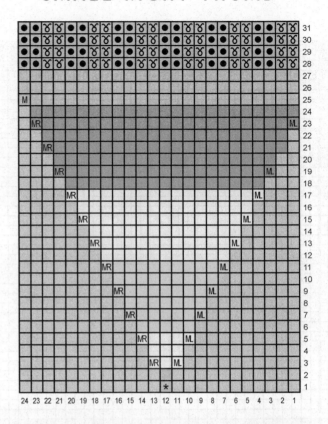

MEDIUM LEFT THUMB

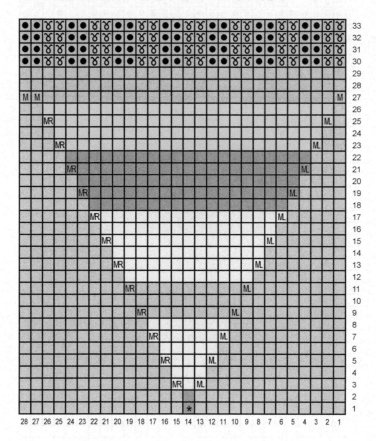

MEDIUM RIGHT THUMB

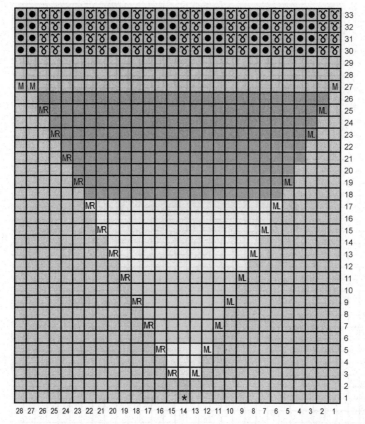

LARGE LEFT THUMB

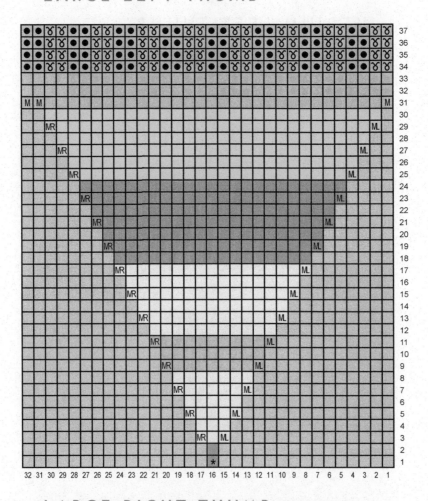

LARGE RIGHT THUMB

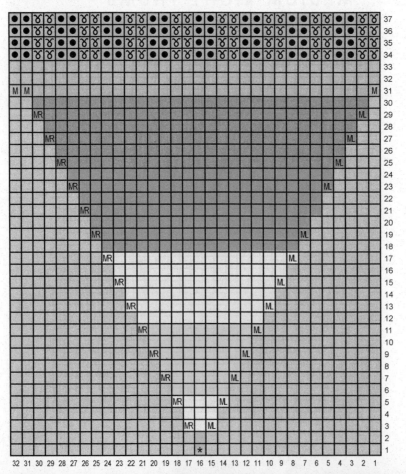

NOUGAT

So now you've tried your hand at stripes – are you looking for something a little stronger? Why not give Nougat a shot?

Nougat is the perfect introduction to the world of colourwork knitting — there's enough colour changes and pattern to keep things looking suitably complicated, but the pattern is so simple and logical in its progression that after a few repeats you might just find that you have it memorized (well, you might have to look at it when you get to the thumbs and fingertip decreases but that's perfectly understandable).

SIZES

Women's S (M, L); shown in size M

FINISHED MEASUREMENTS

Length 8.75 (9.75, 11.63)" / 22.2 (24.8, 29.54) cm

Palm Circumference 7 (8, 9.5)" / 17.78 (20.32, 24.13) cm

MATERIALS

Knit Picks Palette (100% wool; 231 yds / 211 m per 50g ball)

» [MC] Puma Heather; 1 ball

» [CCA] Rose Hip; partial ball

» [CCB] Pimento; partial ball

» [CCD] Pennyroyal; partial ball

1 set US #2 / 2.75mm double-point needles

Stitch marker (optional)
Waste yarn or stitch holder
Yarn needle

GAUGE

8 sts = 1" / 2.54 cm in stranded colourwork pattern

8 rnds = 1" / 2.54 cm in stranded colourwork pattern

PATTERN NOTES

You will get to the point where you can look at your knitted work-in-progress and know where you're at in the pattern. This is called "reading your knitting" and it's one of the most valuable skills you can learn as a knitter.

The other skill that I would strongly urge you to try when working this pattern is knitting with both hands. For this pattern you will want to hold the yarn you're working the background with in your right hand (and knitting it English) and the yarn you're using to work the little flower motifs in you left hand (and knitting it Continental). You'll find that the flowers stand out a little more (as Continental knitting is usually slightly looser than English knitting,) and hang together a little better.

This skill, like the skill of "reading" your knitting, is something that only comes with time and experience - but once you polish off a pair of Nougat mittens you should be well on your way, if not a hands-down pro! It only took me making one pair of colourwork mittens in this way to get used to both techniques.

PATTERN

Cuff

Using CCA, CO 56 (64, 76) sts using the Long-tail cast on, or any other stretchy cast on. Distribute sts evenly across 4 needles—14 (16, 19) sts on each. The needles will now be known as N1, 2, 3 and 4 respectively. Being careful not to twist sts, prepare to beg to work in the rnd, working the cuff as follows:

Rnd 1: [K2tbl, p2] repeat across all sts.

Rep Rnd 1 for the next 7 (9, 11) rnds, for a total of 8 (10, 12) rnds of ribbing. Now, work all sts of the next rnd in St st.

Mitten Body

Work from chart S, M or L, following from right to left. Please note that the chart shows every st in every rnd. Continue working from your chosen chart until Rnd 29 (29, 31) where there is a mark denoting thumb placement.

THUMB PLACEMENT

For LH mitten: Work across all sts on N1, 2 and 3. Work the first 2 (3, 5) sts on N4. Using a 15"/38 cm piece of waste yarn k the next 9 (10, 11) sts on N4. Slip these sts back onto the LH needle and continue to work in pattern. Work the last 3 sts rem on N4 - 14 (16, 19) sts remain on N4.

For RH mitten: Work across N1 and N2. Knit the first 3 sts on N3. Using the 15"/38 cm piece

of waste yarn k the next 9 (10, 11) sts on N3. Slip these sts back onto the LH needle and continue to work in pattern. Work the remaining sts on N3 - 14 (16, 19) sts rem on N3. Work across all sts on N4 in pattern.

NOTE: If making fingerless mittens please work from the following directions. If making regular mittens please skip the following directions and proceed to the Regular Mittens section.

FINGERLESS MITTENS

Work to the end of Rnd 32, or until mitten reaches just below the recipient's knuckles (or desired length.) Working with MC only work the next 2 rnds in St st. Prepare to complete fingerless mitten body as follows:

Rnds 1–5: Using MC, work [k2tbl, p2] rib across all sts.

Bind off all sts loosely.

FINGERLESS MITTEN THUMB

Pick up 9 (10, 11) sts both above and below the sts held on the waste yarn, along with 4 total sts from the sides of the thumbhole for a total of 22 (24, 26) sts, discarding the waste yarn when finished.

Arrange the sts across 4 needles as follows:

- » Small size: N1 - 5 sts, N2 - 6 sts, N3 - 5 sts, N4 - 6 sts.
- » Medium size: 6 sts on all needles.

- » Large size: N1 - 6 sts, N2 - 7 sts, N3 - 6 sts, N4 - 7 sts.

Work the thumb, starting from the outer lower corner and working across the front of the thumb. This first needle will be known as N1, with the other needles known as N2, N3 and N4 respectively. Work the thumb as follows:

Rnd 1: With MC, k all sts.

Continue working Rnd 1 until thumb reaches just below the recipient's thumb joint, or desired length, working to the end of N4. Complete thumb as follows:

Small and Large sizes only:

Rnd 1: [K2tbl, p2] repeat to last 2 sts, k2tog.
Rnd 2: [K2tbl, p2] repeat to last 5 sts, k2tbl, p1, p2tog.
Rnds 3 - 4: [K2tbl, p2] rib across all sts.

Medium size only:

Rnds 1–4: Using MC only, work [k2tbl, p2] rib across all sts.

Bind off all sts loosely. The fingerless mitten thumb is complete. Proceed to Finishing directions below.

Mitten Body (continued)

Continue working from your chart until rnd 53 (59, 71) where the finger decreases begin. Please note: The finger decreases can be successfully executed working only from your chart or from the instructions below (or both.)

FINGER DECREASES

Decrease for the fingertips as follows:

» N1: Slip the first st, k1, psso, work across all remaining sts in pattern.

» N2: Work across all sts in pattern until 2 sts remain, k2tog.

» N3: Slip the first st, k1, psso, work across all remaining sts in pattern.

» N4: Work across all sts in pattern until 2 sts remain, k2tog.

Repeat this until 16 sts remain, working the final rnd to the end of N4. There should now be 4 sts on each needle – 16 sts remain. Slip all sts from N2 onto N1, and all sts from N4 onto N3 – 8 sts on each needle. Break MC yarn, leaving a generous amount to graft remaining sts. Kitchener Stitch the top of the mitten closed.

Thumb

Pick up 9 (10, 11) sts both above and below the sts held on the waste yarn, along with a total of 4 sts from the sides of the thumbhole for a total of 22 (24, 26) sts, discarding the waste yarn when finished.

Divide sts across needles as follows:

» Small size: N1 – 5 sts, N2 – 6 sts, N3 – 5 sts, N4 – 6 sts.

» Medium size: 6 sts on all needles.

» Large size: N1 – 6 sts, N2 – 7 sts, N3 – 6 sts, N4 – 7 sts.

Begin working thumb, starting from the outer lower corner and working across the front of the thumb. Work the thumb as follows:

Rnd 1: With MC, knit all stitches.

Continue working rnd 1 until thumb reaches to about the

tip of the recipient's thumb, or desired length, working to the end of N4. Work thumb decreases as follows:

» N1: Slip 1 st, k1, psso, work all remaining sts in pattern.

» N2: Work all sts in pattern until 2 sts remain, k2tog.

» N3: Slip 1 st, k1, psso, work all remaining sts in pattern.

» N4: Work all sts in pattern until 2 sts remain, k2tog.

Repeat until 8 sts remain – 2 sts on each needle. Break yarn, leaving a generous amount to close up top of mitten. Draw yarn tail through 8 remaining sts several times to close top of thumb.

Finishing

Weave in ends. Place mitten beneath a damp tea towel and press with a hot iron set to the wool setting to steam block.

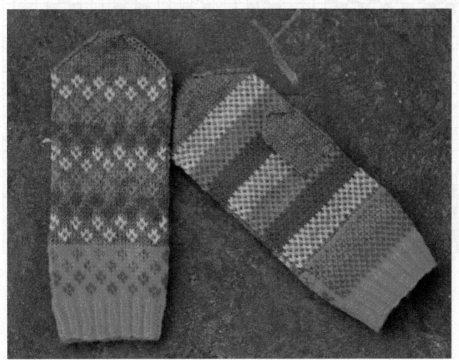

☐ Knit Main Colour

▨ Knit Contrast Colour A

▨ Knit Contrast Colour B

▨ Knit Contrast Colour D

☑ K2tog

◩ Slip 1, k1, psso

☐ Right thumb placement

☐ Left thumb placement

▨ No stitch

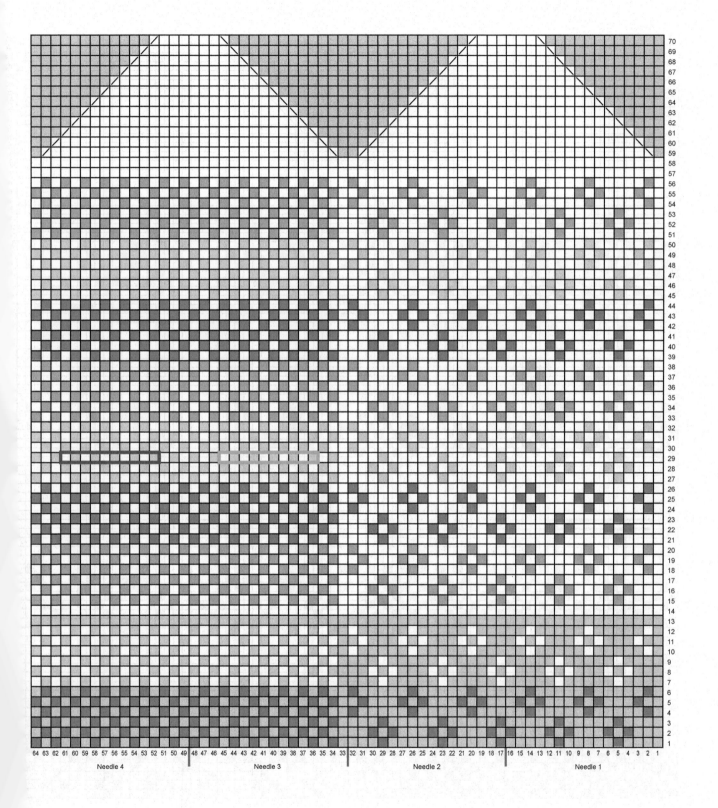

NOUGAT CHART, SIZE L

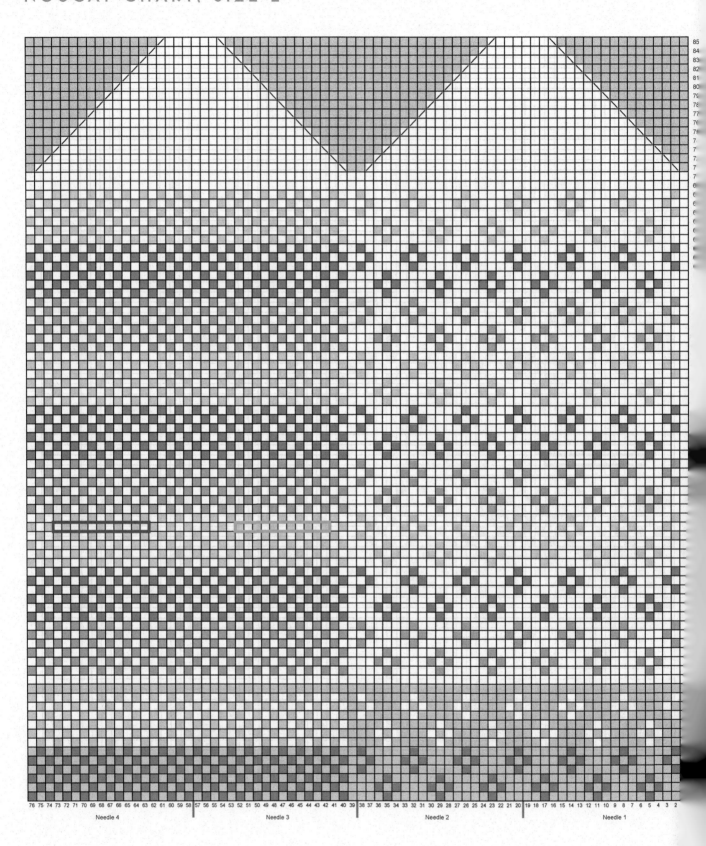

Needle 4   Needle 3   Needle 2   Needle 1

IT IS SOMETIMES A TRICK TO FIND THE BEAUTY IN OUR URBAN environments, but the thing about cities is that even their most mundane corners are places of colour and pattern. While visiting New York City I couldn't help but notice the subway ventilation gratings underfoot. I got caught up in their hypnotic, minimalist rhythm and just had to put them on mittens.

SIZES

Women's M (L); shown in size M

FINISHED MEASUREMENTS

Length 10 (11.23)" / 25.4 (28.5) cm

Palm Circumference 8 (9)" / 20.32 (22.86) cm

MATERIALS

Brooklyn Tweed LOFT (100% Targhee-Columbia wool; 275 yds / 251 m per 50g ball)

» [MC] Snowbound; 1 skein
» [CC] Soot; 1 skein

1 set US #1 / 2.25mm double-point needles

Stitch marker (optional)
Waste yarn, or stitch holder

Yarn needle

GAUGE

9 sts = 1" / 2.54 cm in stranded colourwork pattern

9.75 rnds = 1" / 2.54 cm in stranded colourwork pattern

PATTERN

Cuff

Using MC, CO 72 (80) sts using the Long-tail cast on, or any other stretchy cast on. Distribute sts evenly across 4 needles—18 (20) sts on each. The needles will now be known as N1, 2, 3 and 4 respectively. Being careful not to twist sts, work the cuff in the round as follows:

Rnd 1: [K2tbl, p2] repeat across all sts.

Repeat Rnd 1 for the next 9 (11) rnds, for a total of 10 (12) rnds of ribbing. Work all sts of the next 2 rnds in St st.

Mitten Body

Work from chart M or L, following from right to left. Please note that the chart shows every st in every rnd. Continue working from the chart until Rnd 31 (33) where there is a mark denoting thumb placement.

THUMB PLACEMENT

For LH mitten: Work across all sts on N1. Work the first 5 (6) sts on N2. Using a 15"/38 cm piece of waste yarn knit the next 10 (11) sts on N4. Slip these sts back onto the LH needle and continue to work in pattern. Work the last 3 sts remaining on N2 - 18 (20) sts remain on N2. Work across N3 and 4 in pattern.

For RH mitten: Work across N1 and N2. Knit the first 3 sts on N3. Using the 15" 38 cm piece of waste yarn knit the next 10 (11) sts on N3. Slip these sts back onto the LH needle and continue to work in pattern. Work the remaining sts on N3 - 18 (20) sts remain on N3. Work across all sts on N4 in pattern.

If making fingerless mittens please work from the following directions. If making regular mittens please skip the following directions and proceed to the Regular Mittens section.

FINGERLESS MITTENS

Work to the end of Rnd 39 or until mitten reaches just below the recipient's knuckles, or desired length. With MC only work the next 2 rnds in St st.

Complete fingerless mitten body as follows:

Rnds 3–7: Work [k2tbl, p2] rib across all sts.

Bind off all sts loosely.

FINGERLESS MITTEN THUMB

Pick up 10 (11) sts both above and below the sts held on the waste yarn, along with 4 total sts from either side of the thumbhole for a total of 24 (26) sts, discarding the waste yarn when finished.

Divide the sts across 4 needles as follows:

» Medium - 6 sts on each needle.

» Large - N1 and 3: 6 sts; N2 and 4: 7 st.

Work the thumb, starting from the outer lower corner and working across the front of the thumb. This first needle will be known as N1, with the other needles known as N2, N3 and N4 respectively.

Rnd 1: With MC, k all sts.

Continue working Rnd 1 until thumb reaches just below the recipient's thumb joint, or desired length, working to the end of N4. Complete the thumb as follows:

Medium:

Rnds 1–4: [K2tbl, p2] rib across all sts.

Large:

Rnd 1: [K2tbl, p2] to last 2 sts, k2tog.

Rnd 2: [K2tbl, p2] to last 5 sts, k2tbl, p1, p2tog.

Rnds 3–4: [K2tbl, p2] rib across all sts.

Bind off all sts loosely. Proceed to Finishing directions below.

Mitten Body (continued)

Continue working from your chart until rnd 70 (80), where the finger decreases begin.

FINGER DECREASES

The finger decreases can be successfully executed working only from the chart or from the instructions below (or both.)

» N1: Slip the first st, k1, psso, work across all remaining sts in pattern.

» N2: Work across all sts in pattern until 2 sts remain, k2tog.

» N3: Slip the first st, k1, psso, work across all remaining sts in pattern.

» N4: Work across all sts in pattern until 2 sts remain, k2tog.

Repeat this until 4 sts remain, working the final rnd to the end of N4. Break MC yarn, leaving a generous amount to close up top of mitten. Draw yarn tail through 4 remaining sts several times to close top of mitten.

Thumb

The thumb is worked with MC only.

Pick up 10 (11) sts both above and below the sts held on the waste yarn, along with 4 sts total from either end of the thumbhole for a total of 24 (26) sts, discarding the waste yarn when finished.

Divide the sts across the needles as follows:

» Medium: 6 sts on each needle.

» Large: N1 - 6 sts, N2 - 7 sts, N3 - 6 sts, N4 - 7 sts.

Begin working thumb, starting from the outer lower corner and working across the front of the thumb.

Work the thumb as follows:

Rnd 1: With MC, knit all sts. Continue working Rnd 1 until thumb reaches to about the tip of the recipient's thumb, or desired length, working to the end of N4. Begin thumb decreases as follows:

» N1: Slip 1 st, k1, psso, work all remaining sts in pattern.

» N2: Work all sts in pattern until 2 sts remain, k2tog.

» N3: Slip 1 st, k1, psso, work all remaining st in pattern.

» N4: Work all sts in pattern until 2 sts remain, k2tog.

Repeat until 8 (10) sts remain. Break MC yarn, leaving a generous amount to close up tip of thumb. Draw yarn tail through remaining sts several times to close tip of thumb.

Finishing

Weave in ends. Place mitten beneath a damp tea towel and press with a hot iron set to the wool setting to steam block.

☐	Knit Main Colour
■	Knit Contrast Colour
◩	K2tog
◩	Slip 1, k1, psso
☐	Right thumb placement
☐	Left thumb placement
▨	No stitch

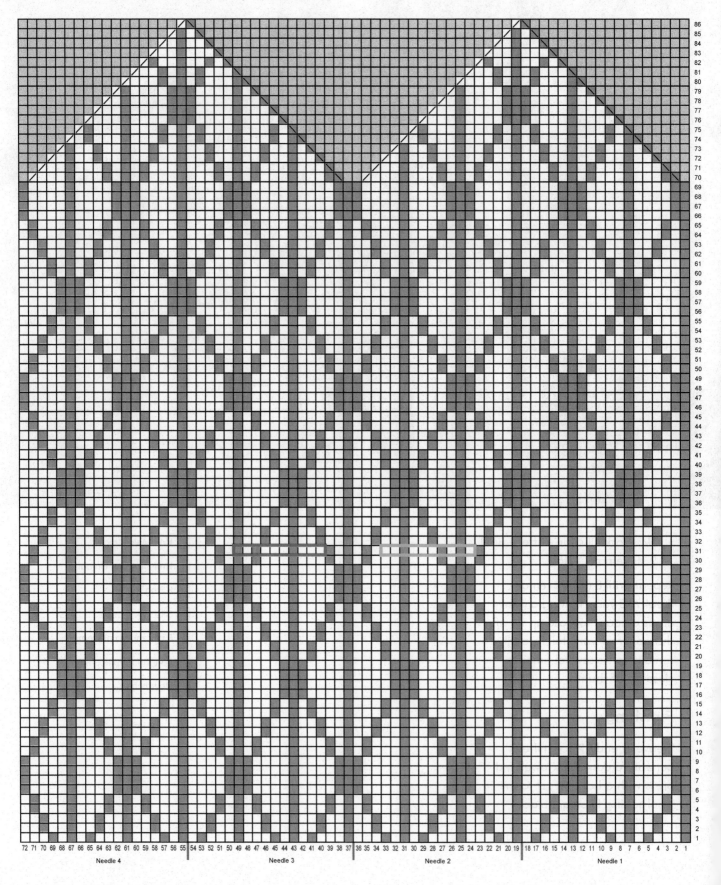

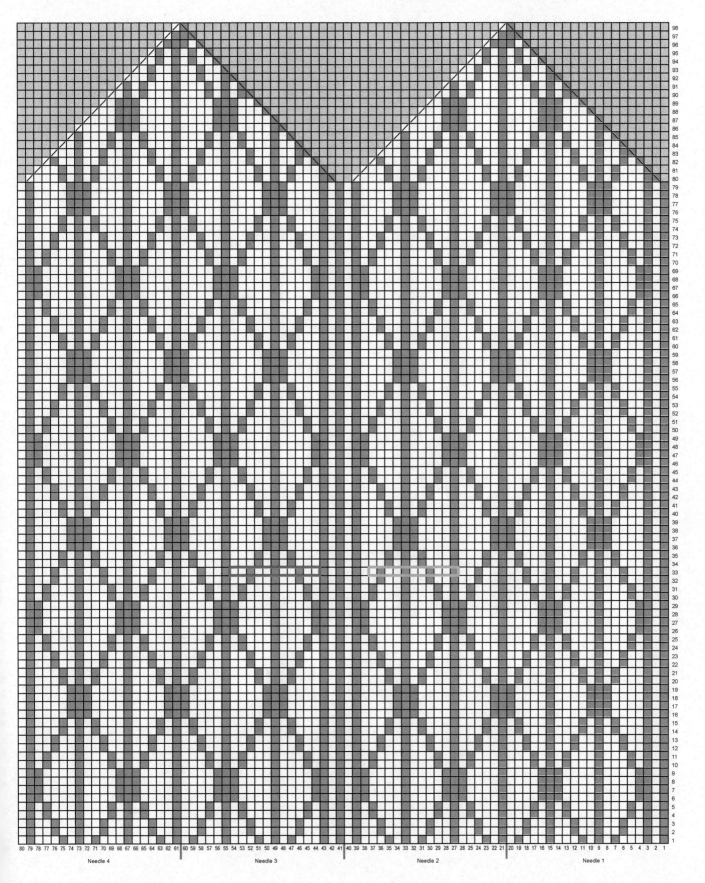

Hello, and welcome to GnomeWatch.

Here at GnomeWatch we are dedicated to ensuring your safety in the presence of—while not malign, still really nosy and rather irritating—gnomes. Gnomes are (mostly) harmless and (mostly) well-meaning, but there is just something about, say, an open tub of cinnamon butter that your average gnome can not resist having a tread through. Yes, that's where those greasy, cinnamon-scented footprints came from. It's not their fault—they were born this way!

When not trotting through condiments gnomes can usually be found hanging out under a nice leafy clump of hostas in the garden. You've been warned.

SIZES

Women's S (M, L); shown in size M

FINISHED MEASUREMENTS

Length 8.55 (10.25, 11.1)" / 21.71 (26, 28.19) cm

Palm Circumference 7 (8, 9)" / 17.78 (20.32, 22.86) cm

MATERIALS

Knit Picks Palette (100% wool; 231 yds / 211 m per 50g ball)

- » [MC] Shire Heather; 1 ball
- » [CCA] Bark; partial ball
- » [CCB] Marine Heather; partial ball
- » [CCD] White; partial ball
- » [CCE] Blush; partial ball
- » [CCF] Pimento; partial ball
- » [CCG] Celadon Heather; partial ball

1 set US #2 / 2.75 mm double-point needles

Stitch marker (optional)
Waste yarn
Yarn needle

GAUGE

8 sts = 1" / 2.54 cm in stranded colour work pattern

8.25 rnds = 1" / 2.54 cm in stranded colourwork pattern

PATTERN

Cuff

Using the MC, CO 56 (64, 72) sts using the Long-tail cast on, or any other stretchy cast on. Distribute sts evenly across 4 needles—14 (16, 18) sts on each. The needles will now be known as N1, 2, 3 and 4 respectively. Being careful not to twist sts, work in the rnd working the cuff as follows:

Rnd 1: [K2tbl, p2] repeat across all sts.

Repeat Rnd 1 for the next 7 (9, 11) rnds, for a total of 8 (10, 12) rnds of ribbing.

Mitten Body

Work from chart S, M or L, following from right to left. Please note that the chart shows every st in every rnd. Continue working from the chart until Rnd 31 (34, 40) where there is a mark denoting thumb placement.

THUMB PLACEMENT

For LH mitten: Work across all sts on N1 and the first 3 (3, 4) sts on N2. Using a 15"/38 cm piece of waste yarn k the next 9 (10, 11) sts on N2. Slip these sts back onto the LH needle and continue to work in pattern across N2 - 14 (16, 18) sts rem on N2.

For RH mitten: Work across N1 and N2. Knit the first 3 (3, 4) sts on N3. Using the 15"/38 cm piece of waste yarn k the next 9 (10, 11) sts on N3. Slip these sts back onto the LH needle and continue to work in pattern across N3 - 14 (16, 18) sts rem on N3. Work across all sts on N4 in pattern.

If making fingerless mittens please work from the following directions. If making regular mittens please skip the following directions and proceed to the Regular Mittens section.

FINGERLESS MITTENS

Work to the end of rnd 47, or until mitten reaches just below the recipient's knuckles, or desired length. Working with MC only work the next 2 rnds in St st.

Rnds 3–7: Using MC only, work [k2tbl, p2] rib across all sts.

Bind off all sts loosely. The fingerless mitten body is complete.

FINGERLESS MITTEN THUMB

Pick up 9 (10, 11) sts both above and below the sts held on the waste yarn, along with 4 total sts from either side of the thumb hole, for a total of 22 (24, 26) sts, discarding the waste yarn when finished.

Divide the sts as follows:

» Small: N1 - 5 sts, N2 - 6 sts, N3 - 5 sts, N4 - 6 sts

» Medium: 6 sts on each needle

» Large: N1 - 6 sts, N2 - 7 sts, N3 - 6 sts, N4 - 7 sts

Work the thumb, starting from the outer lower corner and working across the front of the thumb.

Rnd 1: With MC, k across all sts. Continue working Rnd 1 until thumb reaches just below the recipient's thumb joint or desired length, working to the end of N4. Complete the thumb as follows:

Small and Large sizes only:

Decrease 1 st on N2 and N4 - 20 (24) sts.

All sizes:

Rnds 1–4: Using, work [k2tbl, p2] rib across all sts.

Bind off all sts loosely. The fingerless mitten thumb is complete. Proceed to Finishing directions below.

Mitten Body (continued)

Continue working from the chart until rnd 57 (69, 74), where the finger decreases begin.

FINGER DECREASES

The finger decreases can be successfully executed working only from the chart or from the instructions below (or both.)

The finger decreases are worked with MC only.

All needles: Knit across all sts until 2 sts remain, k2tog.

Continue working rnds in this manner until 12 stitches remain, working the final round to the end of N4. There should now be 3 sts on each needle Break yarn, leaving a generous tail. Using sewing needle draw yarn tail through the 12 remaining live sts to close top of mitten. Prepare to work thumb.

Thumb

Pick up 9 (10, 11) sts both above and below the sts held on the waste yarn, along with 4 total sts from either side of the thumb hole, for a total of 22 (24, 26) sts, discarding the waste yarn when finished.

Divide the sts as follows:

» Small: N1 - 5 sts, N2 - 6 sts, N3 - 5 sts, N4 - 6 sts

» Medium: 6 sts on each needle

» Large: N1 - 6 sts, N2 - 7 sts, N3 - 6 sts, N4 - 7 sts

Begin working thumb, starting from the outer lower corner and working across the front of the thumb.

Work the thumb as follows:

Rnd 1: With MC, k across all sts.

Continue working Rnd 1 until thumb reaches to about the tip of the recipient's thumb (or desired length,) working to the end of N4.

Begin to decrease for the thumb as follows:

Small and Large sizes only:

Decrease 1 st on N2 and 4 – 20 (24) sts

All sizes:

Next rnd:

All 4 needles: knit across all sts until 2 sts remain, k2tog.

Continue working in this manner until 8 sts total remain, working

the final rnd to the end of N4. There should now be 2 sts on each needle. Break yarn, leaving a generous tail. Using sewing needle draw yarn tail through 8 rem live sts to close top of thumb.

Finishing

Weave in ends. Place mitten beneath a damp tea towel and press with a hot iron set to the wool setting to steam block.

CHART KEY

☐ Knit MC
■ Knit CC A
▨ Knit CC B
☐ Knit CC D
▨ Knit CC E
▨ Knit CC F
▨ Knit CC G
☑ K2tog
◩ Slip 1, k1, psso
☐ Right thumb placement
☐ Left thumb placement
▨ No stitch

THUMB CHARTS

Small

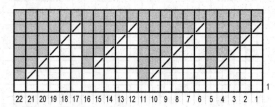

22 21 20 19 18 17 16 15 14 13 12 11 10 9 8 7 6 5 4 3 2 1

Medium

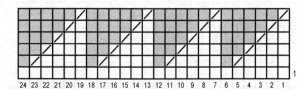

24 23 22 21 20 19 18 17 16 15 14 13 12 11 10 9 8 7 6 5 4 3 2 1

Large

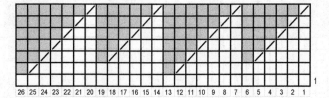

26 25 24 23 22 21 20 19 18 17 16 15 14 13 12 11 10 9 8 7 6 5 4 3 2 1

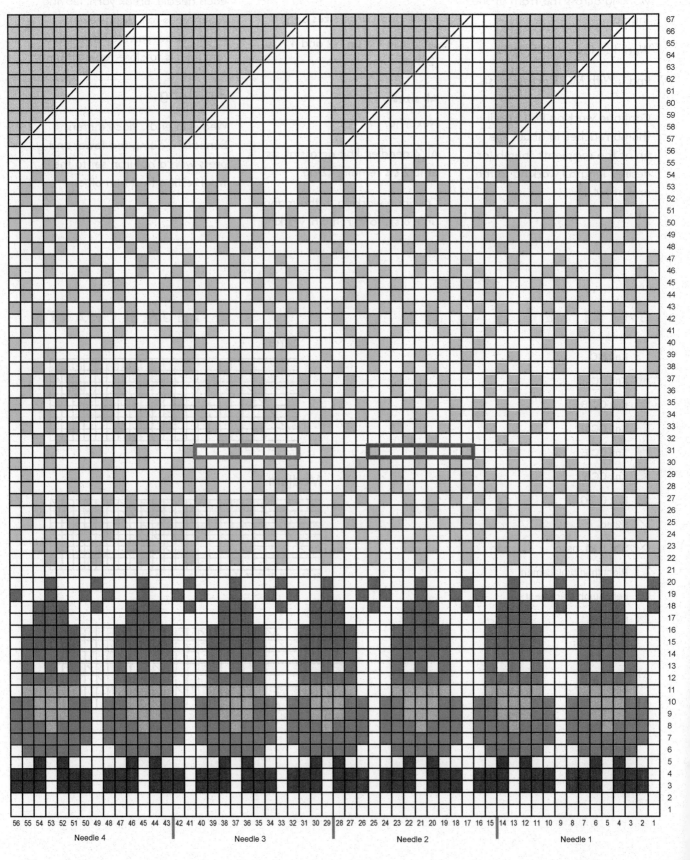

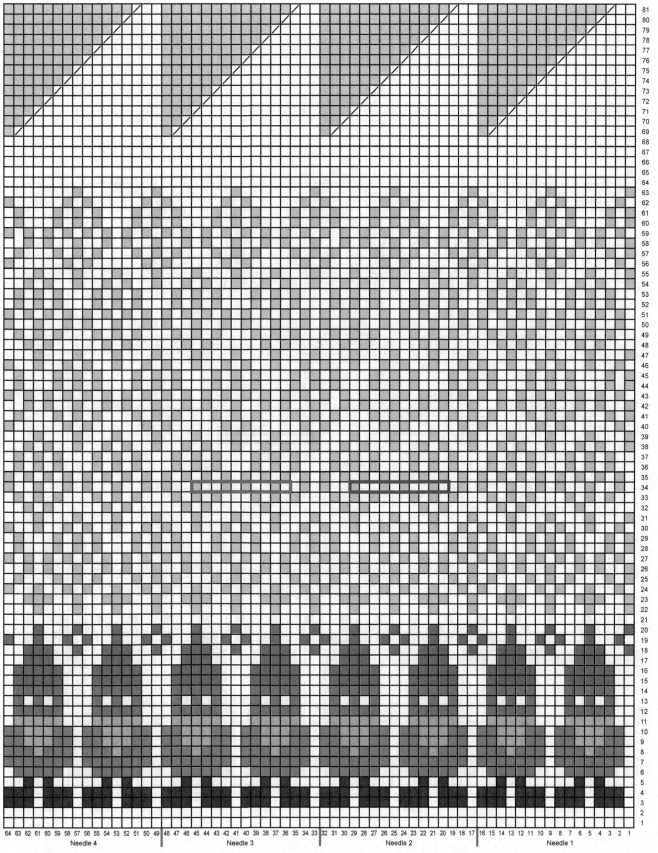

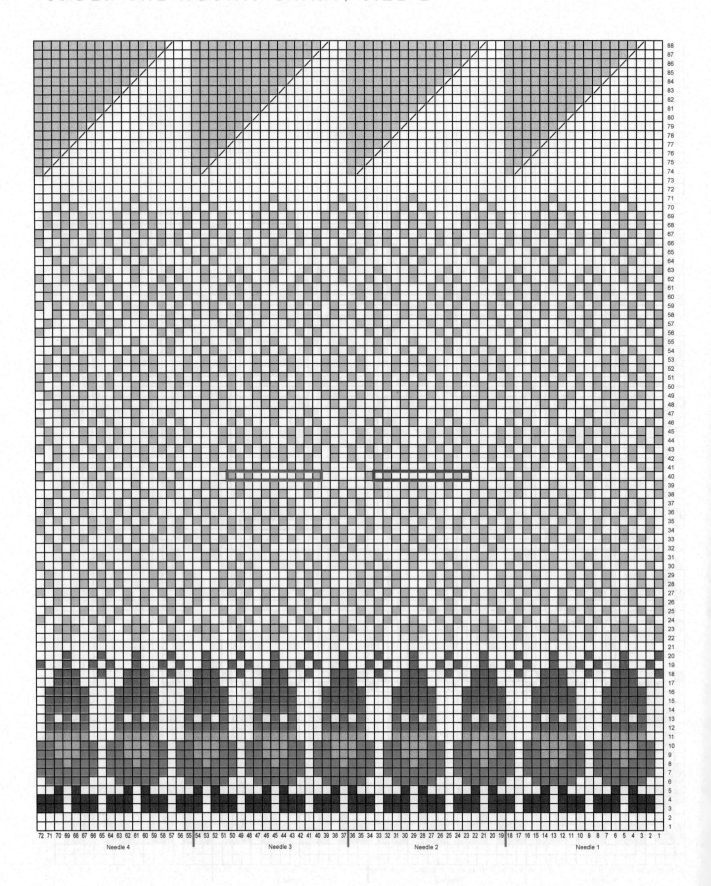

I AM A BIG FAN OF FISH; I LOVE THEIR SOMEWHAT GRUMPY expressions and their rather blank, beady-eyed stares. If there's a body of water chances are someone fishy is about.

Work these mitts for the ichthyophile (or the Pisces) in your life.

SIZES

Women's S (M, L); shown in size M

FINISHED MEASUREMENTS

Length 8.3 (9.5, 11.1)" / 21.08 (24.13, 28.19) cm

Palm Circumference 7 (8, 9)" / 17.8 (20.3, 22.9) cm

MATERIALS

Brooklyn Tweed LOFT (100% Targhee-Columbia wool; 275 yds / 251 m) per 50g ball)

» [MC] Fossil; 1 skein
» [CC] Almanac; 1 skein

1 set US #2 / 2.75 mm double-point needles

Stitch marker (optional)
Waste yarn
Yarn needle

GAUGE

8 sts = 1" / 2.54 cm in stranded colourwork pattern

7.5 rnds = 1" / 2.54 cm in stranded colourwork pattern

PATTERN

Cuff

Using MC, CO 56 (64, 72) sts using the Long-tail cast on, or any other stretchy cast on. Distribute sts evenly across 4 needles—14 (16, 18) sts on each. The needles will now be known as N1, 2, 3 and 4 respectively. Being careful not to twist sts, work the cuff in the rnd, as follows:

Rnd 1: [K2tbl, p2] repeat across all sts.

Repeat Rnd 1 for the next 7 (9, 11) rnds, for a total of 8 (10, 12) rnds of ribbing. Work all sts of the next rnd in St st.

Mitten Body

Work from the chart S, M or L, following from right to left.

Please note that the chart shows every st in every rnd.

Continue working from the appropriate chart until Rnd 25 (29, 33), where there is a mark denoting thumb placement.

THUMB PLACEMENT

For LH mitten: Work across all sts on N1, 2 and 3. Work the first 3 (3, 4) sts on N4. Using a 15"/38 cm piece of waste yarn knit the next 9 (10, 11) sts on N4. Slip these sts back onto the LH needle and continue to work in pattern. Work the last sts remaining on N4 - 14 (16, 18) sts remain on N4.

For RH mitten: Work across N1 and N2. Knit the first 3 sts on N3. Using the 15"/38 cm piece of waste yarn knit the next 9 (10, 11) sts on N3. Slip these sts back onto the LH needle and continue to work in pattern. Work the last 3 sts on N3 - 14 (16, 18) sts rem on N3. Work across all sts on N4 in pattern.

If making fingerless mittens please work from the following

directions. If making regular mittens please skip the following directions and proceed to the Regular Mittens section.

FINGERLESS MITTENS

Work to the end of Rnd 37, or until mitten reaches just below the recipient's knuckles (or desired length.) Working with MC only work the next 2 rnds in St st. Prepare to complete fingerless mitten body as follows:

Rnds 1–5: [K2tbl, p2] repeat across all sts.

Bind off all sts loosely.

FINGERLESS MITTEN THUMB

Pick up 9 (10, 11) sts both above and below the sts held on the waste yarn, along with a total of 4 sts from either side of the thumbhole for a total of 22 (24, 26) sts.

» Small: Divide the sts across 4 needles thus: N1 – 5 sts, N2 – 6 sts, N3 – 5 sts, N4 – 6 sts.

» Medium: Divide the sts evenly across 4 needles, so you have 6 sts on each needle.

» Large: Divide the sts across 4 needles thus: N1 – 6 sts, N2 – 7 sts, N3 – 6 sts, N4 – 7 sts.

Work the thumb, starting from the outer lower corner and working across the front of the thumb.

Rnd 1: With MC, knit all sts.

Continue working Rnd 1 until thumb reaches just below the recipient's thumb joint, or desired length, working to the end of N4.

Next 4 rnds: Work [k2tbl, p2] rib across all sts.

Bind off all sts loosely.

Mitten Body (continued)

Work from the appropriate chart until Rnd 54 (62, 73) where the finger decreases begin.

The finger decreases can be successfully executed working only from the chart or from the instructions below (or both.)

FINGER DECREASES

The finger decreases are worked with MC only. Decrease for the fingertips as follows:

» N1: Slip the first st, k1, psso, knit to end of needle.

» N2: Knit to last two sts, k2tog.

» N3: Slip the first st, k1, psso, knit to end of needle.

» N4: Knit to last two sts, k2tog.

Repeat this until 20 (20, 24) sts remain, working the final rnd to the end of N4. There should now be 5 (5, 6) sts on each needle. Slip all sts from N2 onto N1, and all sts from N4 onto N3 – 10 (10, 12) sts on each needle. Break yarn, leaving a generous amount to graft remaining sts. Kitchener Stitch the top of the mitten closed.

Thumb

Pick up 9 (10, 11) sts both above and below the sts held on the waste yarn, along with a total of 4 sts from either side of the thumbhole for a total of 22 (24, 26) sts.

» Small: Divide the sts across 4 needles thus: N1 – 5 sts, N2 – 6 sts, N3 – 5 sts, N4 – 6 sts.

» Medium: Divide the sts evenly across 4 needles, so you have 6 sts on each needle.

» Large: Divide the sts across 4 needles thus: N1– 6 sts, N2 – 7 sts, N3 – 6 sts, N4 – 7 sts.

Begin working thumb, starting from the outer lower corner and working across the front of the thumb. The needles will be known as N1, 2, 3 and 4 respectively. Work the thumb as follows:

Rnd 1: With MC, knit all sts. Continue working Rnd 1 until thumb reaches to about the tip of the recipient's thumb or desired length, working to the end of N4. Begin thumb decreases as follows:

Small and Large sizes only:

Decrease 1 st on N2 and N4 – 20 (24 sts)

» N1: Slip the first st, k1, psso, knit to end of needle.

» N2: Knit to last two sts, k2tog.

» N3: Slip the first st, k1, psso, knit to end of needle.

» N4: Knit to last two sts, k2tog.

Repeat until 8 sts remain – 2 sts on each needle. Slip all sts from N2 to N1 and all sts from N4 onto N3 – 4 sts remaining on each needle. Break MC yarn, leaving a tail to graft remaining sts.

Kitchener Stitch the top of the thumb closed.

Finishing

Weave in ends. Place mitten beneath a damp tea towel and press with a hot iron set to the wool setting to steam block.

☐ Knit MC

▨ Knit CC

▨ K2tog

◨ Slip 1, k1, psso

☐ Right thumb placement

☐ Left thumb placement

▨ No stitch

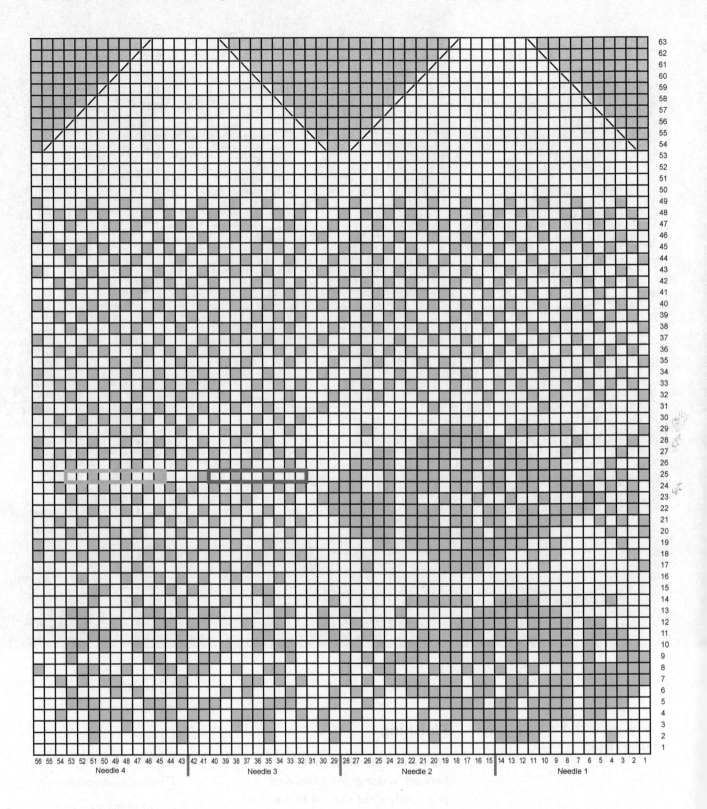

CUPCAKE MITTENS

OH MY, LOOK AT ALL THOSE WEE CUPCAKES! BUT WHICH ONE to sample first? So many tasty choices, but never fear—these woolly cupcake mittens are one hundred percent guilt-free!

Don't let the number of colour changes—and the resulting ends that inevitably go along with them—in these mittens scare you! Remember that you can use as many or as few different colours for your cupcakes as you like.

SIZES

Women's S (M, L); shown in size M

FINISHED MEASUREMENTS

Length 8.56 (9.75, 11.15)" / 21.74 (24.8, 28.32) cm

Palm Circumference 6.6 (8, 9.3)" / 16.74 (20.32, 23.12) cm

MATERIALS

Knit Picks Palette (100% wool; 231 yds/211 m per 50g ball)

» [MC] Bluebell; 1 ball
» [CCA] Custard; partial ball
» [CCB] White; partial ball
» [CCD] Rouge; partial ball
» [CCE] Doe; partial ball
» [CCF] Bark; partial ball
» [CCG] Pimento; partial ball
» [CCH] Cotton Candy; partial ball
» [CCI] Garnet Heather; partial ball

1 set US #1 / 2.25mm double-point needles

Stitch marker (optional)
Waste yarn or stitch holder
Yarn needle

GAUGE

9 sts = 1" / 2.54 cm in stranded colour work pattern

9.25 rnds = 1" / 2.54 cm in stranded colourwork pattern

PATTERN

Cuff

Using MC, CO 60 (72, 84) sts using the Long-tail cast on, or any other stretchy cast on. Distribute sts evenly across 4 needles—15 (18, 21) sts on each. The needles will now be known as N1, 2, 3 and 4 respectively. Being careful not to twist sts, work in the rnd working the cuff as follows:

Rnd 1: [K2tbl, p2] rep across all sts.

Rep Rnd 1 for the next 7 (9, 11) rnds, for a total of 8 (10, 12) rnds of ribbing. Work all sts of the next 2 rnds in St st.

Mitten Body

Work from chart S, M or L, following from right to left. Please note that the chart shows every st in every rnd. Continue working from your chart until Rnd 25 (29, 31) where there is a mark denoting thumb placement.

THUMB PLACEMENT

For LH mitten: Work across all sts on N1. Work the first 3 (3, 4) sts on N2. Using a 15" /38 cm piece of waste yarn k the next 10 (12, 14) sts on N4. Slip these sts back onto the LH needle and continue to work in pattern. Work the remaining sts on N4 - 15 (18, 21) sts remain on N4. Work across N3 and 4 in pattern.

For RH mitten: Work across N1 and N2. Knit the first 3 (3, 4) sts on N3. Using the 15"/38 cm piece of waste yarn, knit the next 10 (12, 14) sts on N3. Slip these sts back onto the LH needle and continue to work in pattern. Work the last 3 (3, 4) sts on N3. Work across all sts on N4 in pattern.

If making fingerless mittens please work from the following directions. If making regular mittens please skip the following directions and proceed to the Regular Mittens section.

FINGERLESS MITTENS

Work to the end of Rnd 54, or until mitten reaches just below the recipient's knuckles, or desired length. Working with MC only work the next 2 rnds in St st. Prepare to complete fingerless mitten body as follows:

Rnds 3–7: [K2tbl, p2] across all sts.

Bind off all sts loosely.

FINGERLESS MITTEN THUMB

Pick up 10 (12, 14) sts both above and below the sts held on the waste yarn, along with 4 sts total on each side of the thumbhole for a total of 24 (28, 32) sts, discarding the waste yarn when finished. Divide the sts evenly across 4 needles—6 (7, 8) sts on each needle. Work the thumb, starting from the outer lower corner and working across the

front of the thumb. This first needle will be known as N1, with the other needles known as N2, N3 and N4 respectively. Work the thumb as follows:

Rnd 1: [K1 MC, k1 CCB], repeat across all sts to the end of N4. Continue working Rnd 1 in the [k1 MC, k1 CCB] rib until thumb reaches just below the recipient's thumb joint, or desired length, working to the end of N4. Complete thumb as follows:

Rnds 1–4: Using MC only, work [k2tbl, p2] across all sts.

Bind off all sts loosely. The fingerless mitten thumb is complete. Proceed to Finishing directions below.

Mitten Body (continued)

Continue working from your chart until Rnd 56 (64, 77), where the finger decreases begin. The finger decreases can be successfully executed working only from your chart or from the instructions below (or both.)

FINGER DECREASES

» N1: Slip the first st, k1, psso, work across all remaining sts in pattern.

» N2: Work across all sts in pattern until 2 sts remain, k2tog.

» N3: Slip the first st, k1, psso, work across all remaining sts in pattern.

» N4: Work across all sts in pattern until 2 sts remain, k2tog.

Repeat this until 24 (24, 48) sts remain, working the final rnd to

the end of N4. There should now be 6 (6, 12) sts on each needle. Slip all sts from N2 onto N1, and all sts from N4 onto N3 - 12 (12, 24) sts on each needle. Break MC yarn, leaving a generous amount to graft remaining sts. Kitchener Stitch the top of the mitten closed.

Thumb

Pick up 10 (12, 14) sts both above and below the sts held on the waste yarn, along with 4 sts total on each side of the thumbhole for a total of 24 (28, 32) sts, discarding the waste yarn when finished. Divide the sts evenly across 4 needles—6 (7, 8) sts on each needle.

Begin working thumb, starting from the outer lower corner and working across the front of the thumb. The needles will be known as N1 2, 3 and 4 respectively. Work the thumb as follows:

Rnd 1: [K1 MC, k1 CCB], repeat across all sts.

Continue working Rnd 1 until thumb reaches to about the tip of the recipient's thumb, or desired length, working to the end of N4. Work thumb decreases as follows:

» N1: Slip 1 st, k1, psso, work all remaining sts in pattern.

» N2: Work all sts in pattern until 2 sts remain, k2tog.

» N3: Slip 1 st, k1, psso, work all remaining st in pattern.

» N4: Work all sts in pattern until 2 sts remain, k2tog.

Repeat until 12 (12, 24) sts remain. Slip all sts from N2 to N1 and all sts from N4 onto N3 – 6 (6, 12) sts rem on each needle. Break yarn, leaving a tail to graft remain sts. Using MC yarn, Kitchener Stitch the top of the thumb closed.

Finishing

Weave in ends. Place mitten beneath a damp tea towel and press with a hot iron set to the wool setting to steam block.

☐ Knit MC

☐ Knit CC A

☐ Knit CC B

■ Knit CC D

■ Knit CC E

■ Knit CC F

■ Knit CC G

■ Knit CC H

☐ Knit CC I

◪ K2tog

◪ Slip 1, k1, psso

☐ Right thumb placement

☐ Left thumb placement

■ No stitch

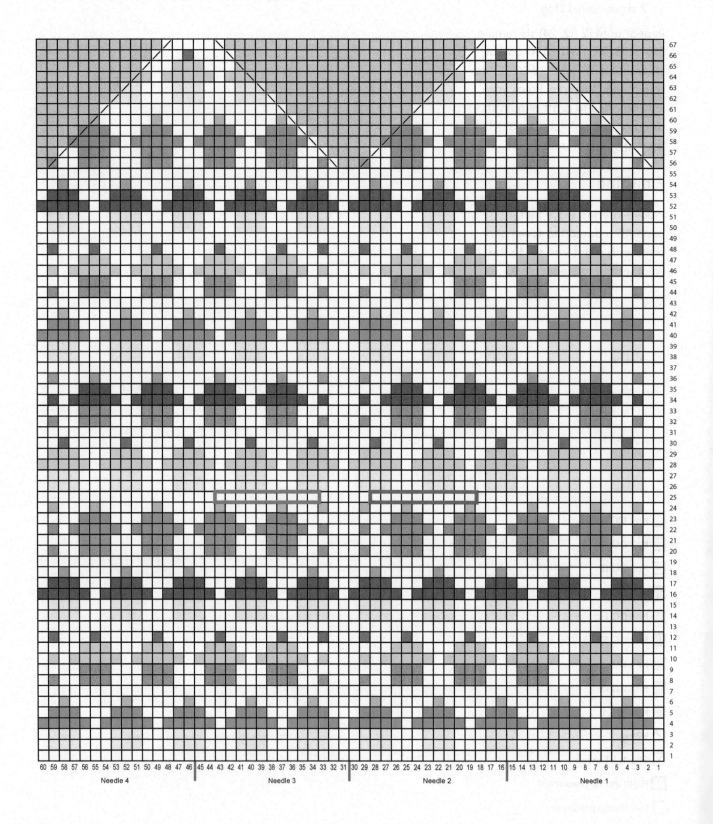

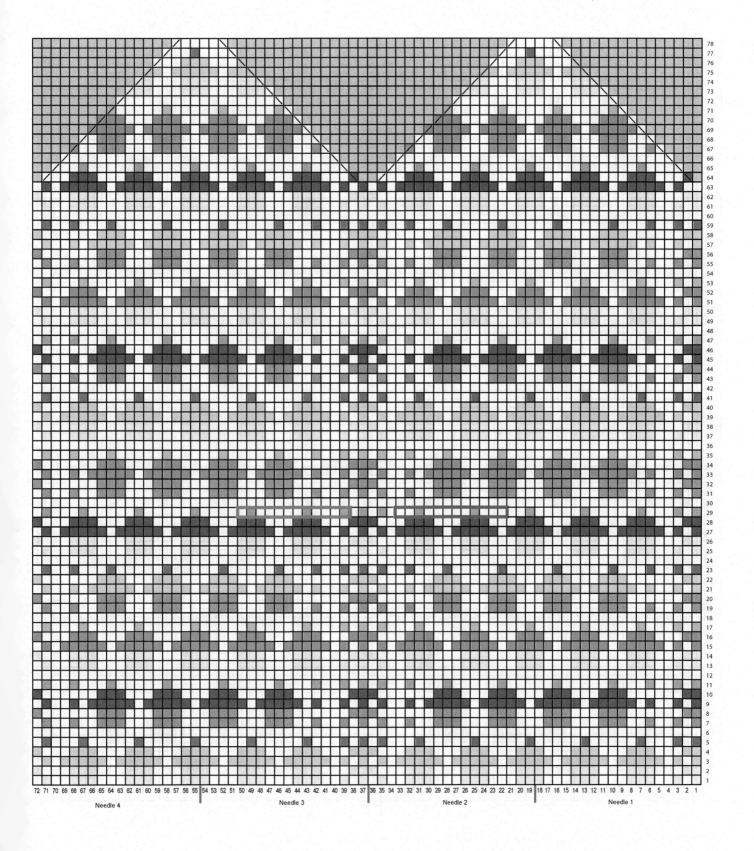

Needle 4   Needle 3   Needle 2   Needle 1

DECADENCE

THESE ART NOUVEAU–INSPIRED MITTENS ARE REMINISCENT OF dark and richly decorated interiors and of the unspeakable delights that may be occurring within. Oh, if these walls could talk..!

Peering through the lush, looping foliage (or are those curls of smoke?) you can just barely make out various instruments of 19th century vice—poppy pods and absinthe spoons. You know you want to work these mittens—go on, you only live once.

SIZES

Women's S (M, L); shown in size M

FINISHED MEASUREMENTS

Length 8.81 (10, 10.65)" / 22.37 (25.4, 27.05) cm

Palm Circumference 8 (9, 10.5)" / 20.32 (22.86, 26.67) cm

MATERIALS

Knit Picks Palette (100% wool; 231 yds / 211 m per 50g ball)

» [MC] Merlot Heather; 1 ball
» [CC] Turmeric; 1 ball

1 set US #1 / 2.25 mm double-point needles

Stitch marker (optional)
Waste yarn or stitch holder
Yarn needle

GAUGE

9 sts = 1" / 2.54 cm in stranded colourwork pattern

9.25 rnds = 1" / 2.54 cm in stranded colourwork pattern

PATTERN

Cuff

Using the MC, CO 56 (72, 84) sts using the Long-tail cast on, or any other stretchy cast on.

Distribute sts evenly across 4 needles - 16 (18, 21) sts on each. The needles will now be known as N1, 2, 3 and 4 respectively. Being careful not to twist sts, work in the rnd working the cuff as follows:

Rnd 1: [K2tbl, p2], repeat across all sts.

Repeat Rnd 1 for the next 7 (9, 11) rnds, for a total of 8 (10, 12) rnds of ribbing. Now, work all sts of the next 2 rnds in St st.

Mitten Body

Work from chart S, M or L, following from right to left. Please note that the chart shows every st in every rnd. Continue working from your chart until Rnd 33 (37, 40) where there is a mark denoting thumb placement.

THUMB PLACEMENT

For LH mitten: Work across all sts on N 1, 2 and 3. Work the first 3 (4, 5) sts on N4. Using a 15"/38 cm piece of waste yarn knit the next 10 (11, 12) sts on N4. Slip these sts back onto the LH needle and continue to work in pattern. Work the remaining sts on N4.

For RH mitten: Work across N1 and N2. Knit the first 3 sts on N3. Using the 15"/38 cm piece of waste yarn knit the next 12 sts on N3. Slip these sts back onto the LH needle and continue to work in pattern. Work the last 3 sts on N3 – 16 (18, 21) sts remain on N3. Work across all sts on N4 in pattern.

Mitten Body (continued)

Continue working from the chart S, M or L until Rnd 61 (70, 73) where the finger decreases begin.

FINGER DECREASES

The finger decreases can be successfully executed working only from your chart or from the instructions below (or both.)

Decreases for the fingertips as follows:

» N1: Slip the first st, k1, psso, work across all remaining sts in pattern.

» N2: Work across all sts in pattern until 2 sts remain, k2tog.

» N3: Slip the first st, k1, psso, work across all remaining sts in pattern.

» N4: Work across all sts in pattern until 2 sts remain, k2tog.

Repeat this until 20 sts remain, working the final rnd to the end of N4. There should now be 5 sts on each n (20 sts rem.) Slip all stitches from N2 onto N1, and all sts from N4 onto N3 (10 sts on each needle). Break yarn, leaving a generous amount to graft remaining sts. Using MC yarn, Kitchener Stitch the top of the

mitten closed. Prepare to work thumb.

Thumb

Pick up 10 (11, 12) sts both above and below the sts held on the waste yarn, along with 4 sts total from either side of the thumb-hole, for a total of 24 24 (26, 28) sts, discarding the waste yarn when finished. Divide the stitches evenly across 4 needles - 6 sts on each needle. Pick up 4 sts at either side of the thumbhole—1 each at beg of N1 and 3, and 1 each at end of N2 and 4 - 28 sts total—7 sts on each needle.

Divide the sts across 4 needles as follows:

» Small - 6 sts on each needle.

» Medium - 6 sts on N1 and N3, 7 sts on N2 and N4.

» Large - 7 sts on each needle.

Begin working thumb, starting from the outer lower corner and working across the front of the thumb.

Work the thumb as follows:

Rnd 1: [K1 MC, k1 CC], repeat across all sts.

Continue working Rnd 1 until thumb reaches to about the tip of the recipient's thumb (or desired length,) working to the end of N4.

THUMB DECREASES

» N1: Slip 1 st, k1, psso, work all remaining sts in pattern.

» N2: Work all sts in pattern until 2 sts remaining, k2tog.

» N3: Slip 1 st, k1, psso, work all remaining sts in pattern.

» N4: Work all sts in pattern until 2 sts remain, k2tog.

Repeat until 8 sts remain - 2 sts on each needle. Slip all sts from N2 to N1 and all sts from N4 onto N3 - 4 sts remain on each needle. Break yarn, leaving a tail to graft rem sts. Kitchener Stitch the top of the thumb closed.

Finishing

Weave in ends. Place mitten beneath a damp tea towel and press with a hot iron set to the wool setting to steam block.

▢ Knit MC

▨ Knit CC

◪ K2tog

◪ Slip 1, k1, psso

▢ Right thumb placement

▢ Left thumb placement

◼ No stitch

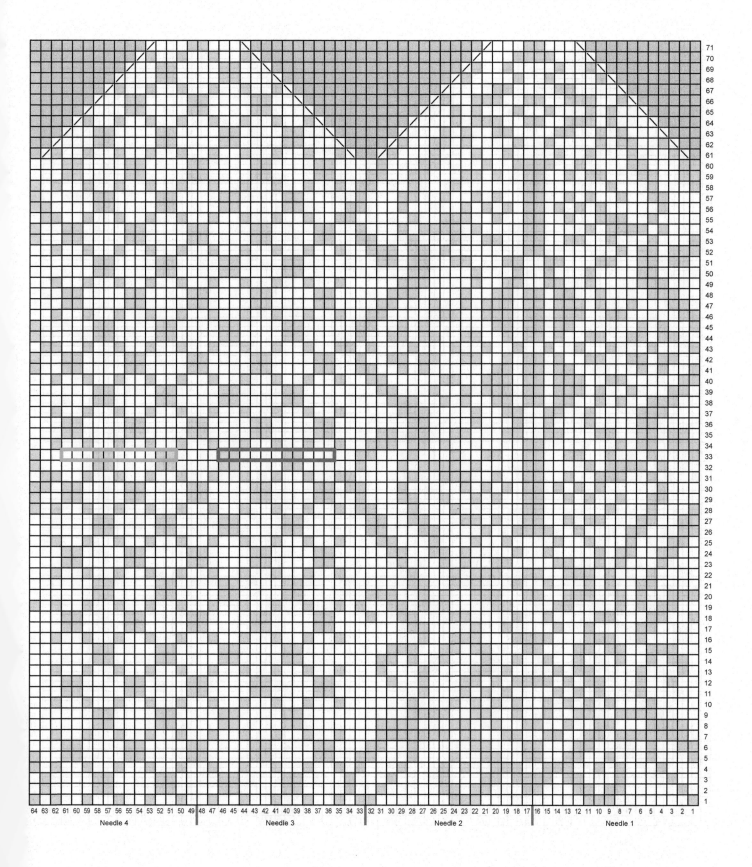

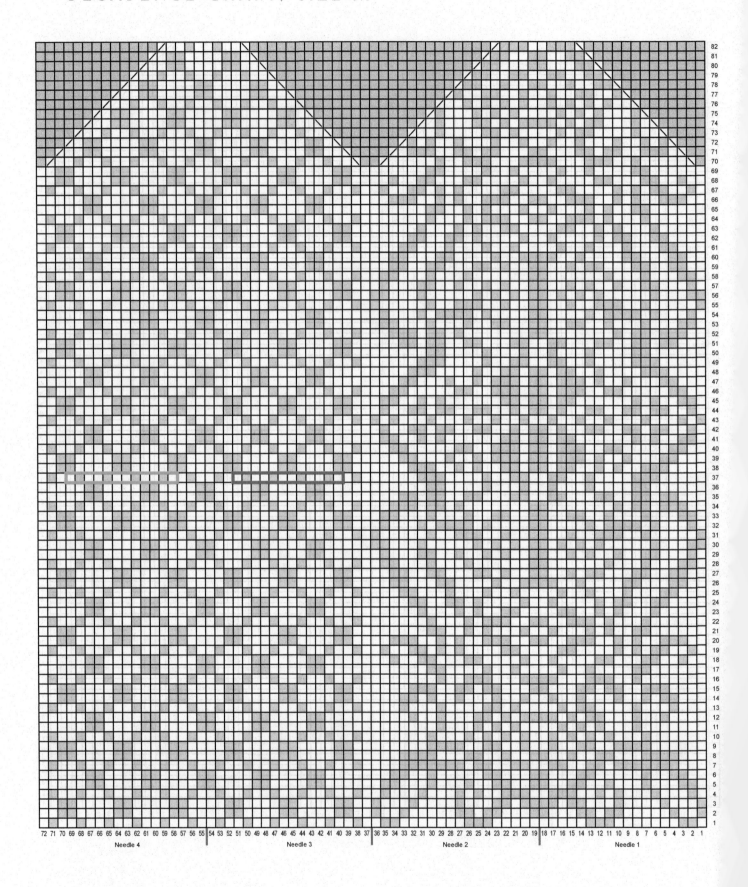

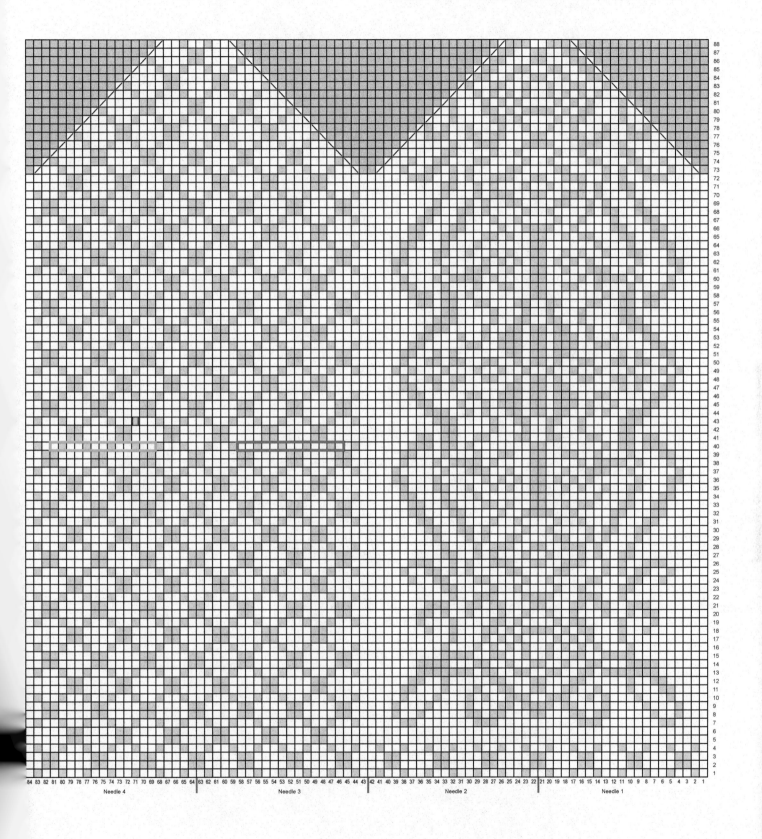

PETOSKEY STONES ARE THE FOSSILIZED REMAINS OF ANCIENT coral beds that have been tumbled by the waves of Lake Michigan for millions of years. The first time I saw one I couldn't wait to see how its markings would translate into a mitten. Though the pattern has been necessarily simplified, the beauty of the fossils they emulate remains.

SIZES

Women's S (M, L); shown in size M

FINISHED MEASUREMENTS

Length 9.05 (9.75, 11.4)" / 23 (24.8, 28.95) cm

Palm Circumference 7 (8, 9.3)" / 17.78 (20.32, 23.62) cm

MATERIALS

Knit Picks Palette (100% wool; 231 yds / 211 m per 50g ball)

» [MC] Lynx Heather; 1 ball
» [CC] Hare Heather; 1 ball

1 set US #1 / 2.25mm double-point needles

Stitch marker (optional)
Waste yarn or stitch holder
Yarn needle

GAUGE

9 sts = 1" / 2.54 cm in stranded colour work pattern

8.5 rnds = 1" / 2.54 cm in stranded colourwork pattern

PATTERN

Cuff

Using MC, CO 64 (72, 84) sts using the Long-tail cast on, or any other stretchy cast on. Distribute sts evenly across 4 needles—16 (18, 21) sts on each. The needles will now be known as N1, 2, 3 and 4 respectively. Being careful not to twist sts, prepare to beg to work in the rnd working the cuff as follows:

Rnd 1: [K2tbl, p2], repeat across all sts.

Repeat Rnd 1 for the next 7 (9, 11) rnds, for a total of 8 (10, 12) rnds of ribbing. Work all sts of the next 2 rnds in St st.

Mitten Body

Work from chart S, M or L following from right to left. Please note that the chart shows every st in every rnd. Continue working from your chart until Rnd 26 (27, 30) where there is a mark denoting thumb placement.

THUMB PLACEMENT

For LH mitten: Work across all sts on N 1, 2 and 3. Work the first 3 (3, 4) sts on N4. Using a 15"/38 cm piece of waste yarn knit the next 10 (12, 14) sts on N4. Slip these sts back onto the LH needle and continue to work in pattern to the end of the needle - 16 (18, 21) sts remain on N4.

For RH mitten: Work across N1 and N2. Knit the first 3 sts on N3. Using the 15"/38 cm piece of waste yarn knit the next 10 (12, 14) sts on N3. Slip these sts back onto the LH needle and continue to work in pattern to the end of the needle - 16 (18, 21) sts rem on N3. Work across all sts on N4 in pattern.

If making fingerless mittens please work from the following

directions. If making regular mittens please skip the following directions and proceed to the Mitten Body (continued) section.

FINGERLESS MITTENS

Work to the end of Rnd 36, or until mitten reaches just below the recipient's knuckles (or desired length.) Working with MC only work the next 2 rnds in St st. Prepare to complete fingerless mitten body as follows:

Rnds 3–7: Work [k2tbl, p2] across all sts.

Bind off all sts loosely.

FINGERLESS MITTEN THUMB

Pick up 10 (12, 14) sts both above and below the sts held on the waste yarn, along with 4 sts total from either side of the thumb hole for a total of 24 (28, 32) sts, discarding the waste yarn when finished. Divide the sts evenly across 4 needles—6 (7, 8) sts on each needle. Prepare to work thumb, starting from the outer lower corner and working across the front of the thumb. This first needle will be known as N1, with the other needles known as N2, N3 and N4 respectively. Work the thumb as follows:

Rnd 1: With MC, knit all sts.

Continue working Rnd 1 until thumb reaches just below the recipient's thumb joint (or desired length,) working to the end of N4.

Rnds 1–4: [K2tbl, p2] rib across all sts.

Bind off all sts loosely. Proceed to Finishing directions below.

Mitten Body (continued)

Continue working from your chart until Rnd 59 (63, 74) where the finger decreases begin.

The finger decreases can be successfully executed working only from the chart or from the instructions below (or both.)

FINGER DECREASES

Decrease for the fingertips as follows:

» N1: Slip the first st, k1, psso, work across all remaining sts in pattern.

» N2: Work across all sts in pattern until 2 sts remain, k2tog.

» N3: Slip the first st, k1, psso, work across all remaining sts in pattern.

» N4: Work across all sts in pattern until 2 sts remain, k2tog.

Repeat this until 20 sts remain, working the final rnd to the end of N4. There should now be 5 sts on each needle. Slip all sts from N2 onto N1, and all sts from N4 onto N3 - 10 sts on each needle. Break yarn, leaving a generous amount to graft remaining sts. Kitchener Stitch the top of the mitten closed.

Thumb

Pick up 10 (12, 14) sts both above and below the sts held on the waste yarn, along with 4 total sts from either side of the thumb hole for a total of 24 (28, 32) sts,

discarding the waste yarn when finished. Divide the sts evenly across 4 needles - 6 (7, 8) sts on each needle.

Begin working thumb, starting from the outer lower corner and working across the front of the thumb. The needles will be known as N1, 2, 3 and 4 respectively. Work the thumb as follows:

Rnd 1: With MC, knit all sts.

Continue working Rnd 1 until thumb reaches to about the tip of the recipient's thumb, or desired length, working to the end of N4. Work thumb decreases as follows:

» N1: Slip 1 st, k1, psso, work all remaining sts in pattern.

» N2: Work all sts in pattern until 2 sts remain, k2tog.

» N3: Slip 1 sts. k1, psso, work all remaining st in pattern.

» N4: Work all sts in pattern until 2 sts remain, k2tog.

Repeat until 8 sts remain. Break yarn, leaving a generous amount to close up top of mitten. Draw yarn tail through 8 remaining sts several times to close top of thumb.

Finishing

Weave in ends. Place mitten beneath a damp tea towel and press with a hot iron set to the wool setting to steam block.

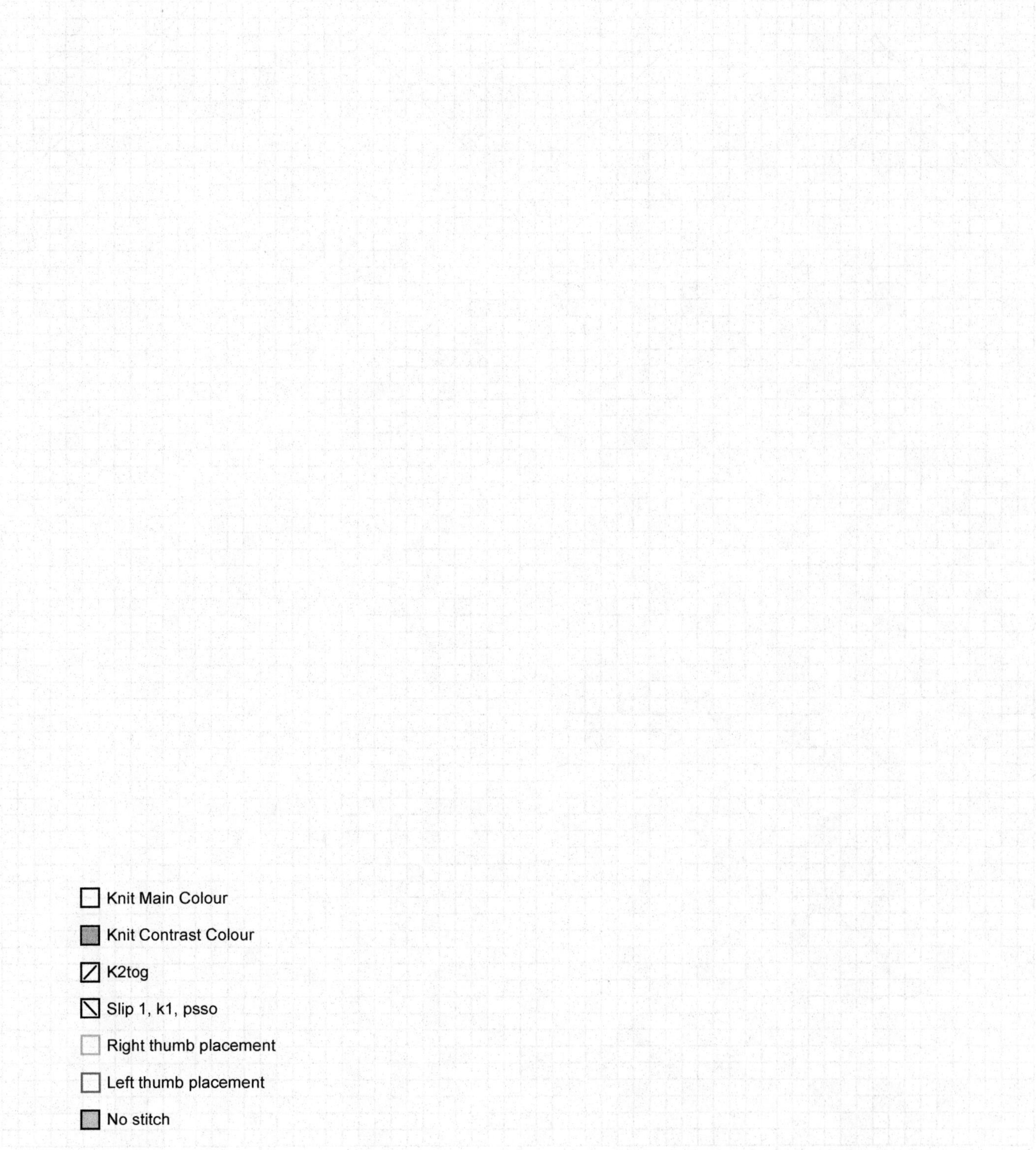

☐ Knit Main Colour

▨ Knit Contrast Colour

◩ K2tog

◪ Slip 1, k1, psso

☐ Right thumb placement

☐ Left thumb placement

▨ No stitch

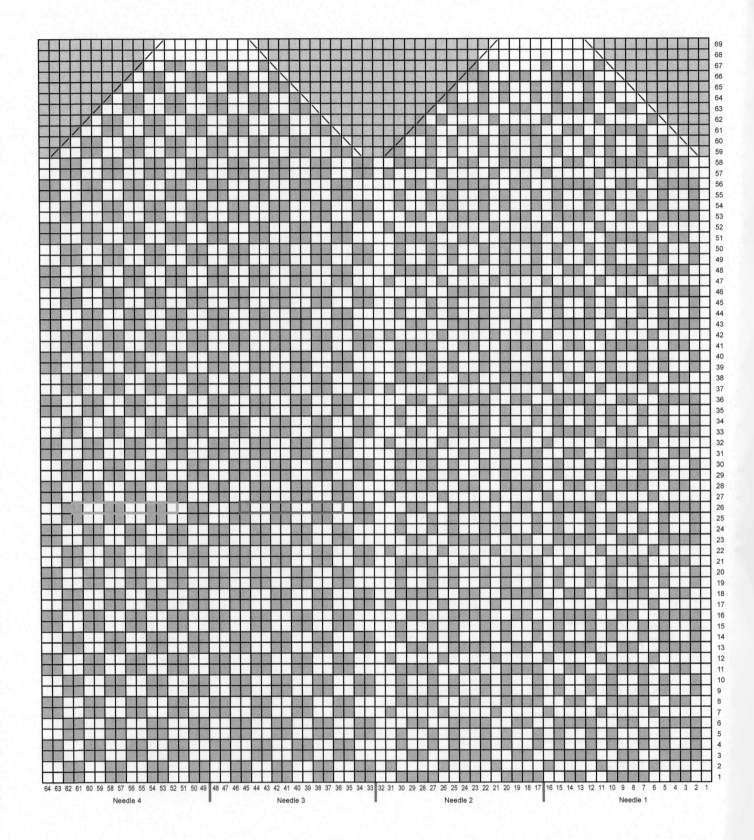

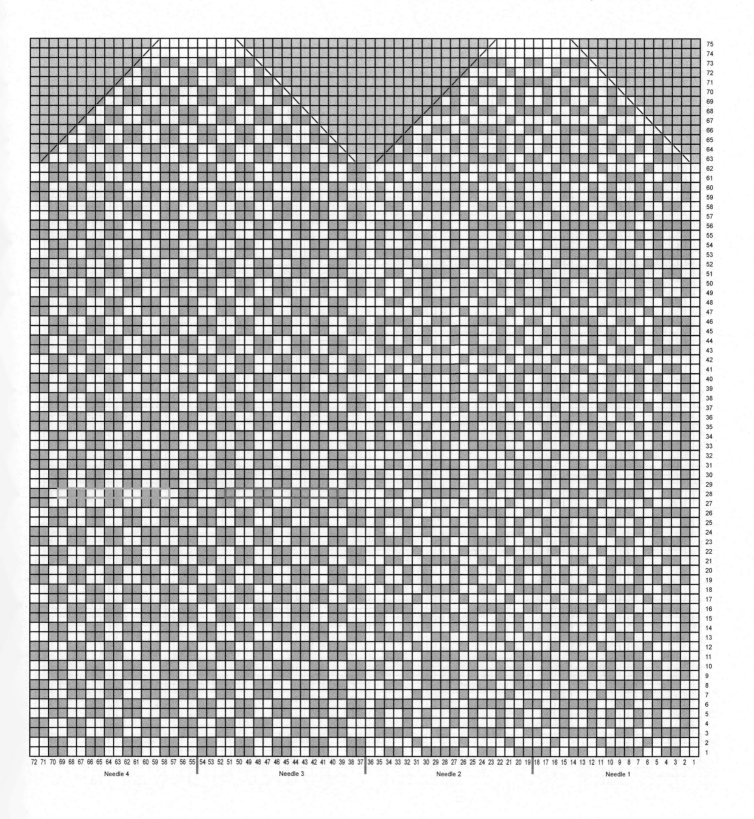

THE GIRL WITH THE
PREFABRICATED HEART

> OH VENUS WAS BORN OUT OF SEA FOAM
> Oh Venus was born out of brine
> But the goddess today if she is grade A
> Is assembled upon the assembly line...

Ideas for mittens can come from anywhere, and the inspiration doesn't even need to be visual. These were inspired by lyrics from the above song, The Real Tuesday Weld's version of "The Girl with the Pre-Fabricated Heart." This parable of love and perfection in the age of plastic originally appears in Hans Richter's 1947 surrealist film DREAMS THAT MONEY CAN BUY. On these mittens I've tried to convey the image of the classical goddess as she might appear had she been imagined in the 20th century era of impersonal mass production.

SIZES

Women's M (L); shown in size M

FINISHED MEASUREMENTS

Length 9 (9.86)" / x 22.9 (25.04) cm

Palm Circumference 8 (8.8)" / 20.32 (22.35) cm

MATERIALS

Brooklyn Tweed LOFT (100% Targhee-Columbia wool; 275 yds / 251 m per 50g ball)

» [MC] Bird Book; 1 skein

» [CC] Camper; 1 skein

1 set US #1 / 2.25mm double-point needles

Stitch marker (optional)
Waste yarn or stitch holder

Yarn needle

GAUGE

9 sts = 1" / 2.54 cm in stranded colour work pattern

9.25 rnds = 1" / 2.54 cm in stranded colourwork pattern

PATTERN

Cuff

Using MC, CO 72 (80) sts using the Long-tail cast on, or any other stretchy cast on. Distribute sts evenly across 4 needles—18 (20) sts on each. The needles will now be known as N1, 2, 3 and 4 respectively. Being careful not to twist sts, work in the rnd working the cuff as follows:

Rnd 1: [K2tbl, p2] repeat across all sts.

Repeat Rnd 1 for the next 9 (11) rnds, for a total of 10 (12) rnds of ribbing. Work all sts of the next 2 rnds in St st. Work body of mitten, from either chart M or L.

Mitten Body

Work from your chart, following from right to left.

Please note that the charts show every st in every rnd.

Continue working from the chart until Rnd 31 (34) where there is a mark denoting thumb placement.

THUMB PLACEMENT

For LH mitten: Work across all sts on N 1, 2 and 3. Work the first 3 sts on N4. Using a 15"/38 cm piece of waste yarn knit the next 12 (14) sts on N4. Slip these sts back onto the LH needle and continue to work in pattern. Work the last 3 sts remaining on N4 - 18 (20) sts remain on N4.

For RH mitten: Work across N1 and N2. Knit the first 3 sts on N3. Using the 15"/38 cm piece of waste yarn knit the next 12 (14) sts on N3. Slip these sts back onto the RH needle and continue to work in pattern. Work the last 3 sts on N3 - 18 (20) sts remain on N3. Work across all sts on N4 in pattern.

Mitten Body (continued)

Continue working from your chart until Rnd (64, 70), where the finger decreases begin.

FINGER DECREASES

The finger decreases can be successfully executed working only from your chart or from the instructions below (or both.)

Decrease for the fingertips as follows:

» N1: Slip the first st, k1, psso, work across all remaining sts in pattern.

» N2: Work across all sts in pattern until 2 sts remain, k2tog.

» N3: Slip the first st, k1, psso, work across all remaining sts in pattern.

» N4: Work across all sts in pattern until 2 sts remain, k2tog.

Repeat this until 20 sts remain, working the final rnd to the end of N4. There should now be 5 sts on each needle. Slip all sts from N2 onto N1, and all sts from N4 onto N3 - 10 sts on each needle. Break yarn, leaving a generous amount to graft remaining sts. Kitchener Stitch the top of the mitten closed.

Thumb

Pick up 12 (14) sts both above and below the sts held on the waste yarn, along with 4 sts total from either side of thumb hole for a total of 28 (32) sts, discarding the waste yarn when finished. Divide the sts evenly across 4 needles - 7 (8) sts on each needle

Begin working thumb, starting from the outer lower corner and working across the front of the thumb. The needles will be known as N1 2, 3 and 4 respectively. Work the thumb as follows:

Rnd 1: With MC, knit all sts.

Continue working Rnd 1 until thumb reaches to about the tip of the recipient's thumb (or desired length,) working to the end of N4. Work thumb decreases as follows:

» N1: Slip 1 st, k1, psso, work all remaining sts in pattern.

» N2: Work all sts in pattern until 2 sts remain, k2tog.

» N3: Slip 1 sts, k1, psso, work all remaining st in pattern.

» N4: Work all sts in pattern until 2 sts remain, k2tog.

Repeat until 8 sts remain. Break yarn, leaving a generous amount to close up top of mitten. Draw yarn tail through 8 remaining sts several times to close top of thumb.

Finishing

Weave in ends. Place mitten beneath a damp tea towel and press with a hot iron set to the wool setting to steam block.

☐	Knit Main Colour
■	Knit Contrast Colour
◪	K2tog
◲	Slip 1, k1, psso
☐	Right thumb placement
☐	Left thumb placement
▨	No stitch

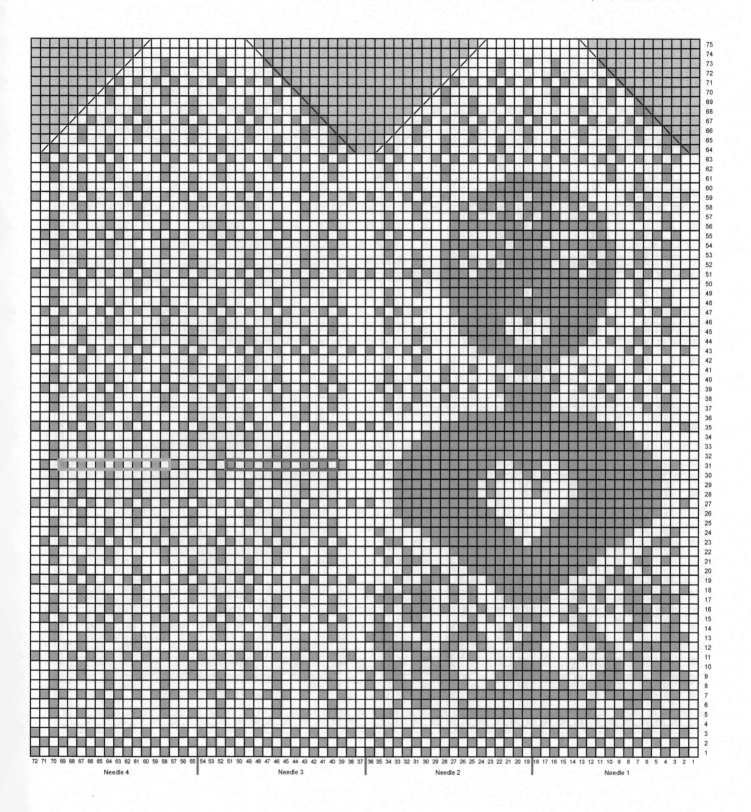

PENGUIN MITTENS

SOME PEOPLE ARE CAT PEOPLE AND SOME PEOPLE ARE DOG PEOPLE, but I'm a bird person. I can never get enough of those little (and not-so-little) feathery guys and their twitchy, sharp-eyed antics. I'd be hard-pressed to choose one species of bird as my favourite but I'm a big fan of penguins. With their fluffy tummies, waddly walk and sophisticated dress sense, penguins are cute, silly and elegant all at the same time—kind of like these mittens.

SIZES

Women's S (M, L); shown in size M

Palm Circumference 7 (8, 9.75)" / 17.78 (20.32, 24.76) cm

FINISHED MEASUREMENTS

Length 8.56 (9.5, 11.03)" / 21.74 (24.13, 28) cm

Palm Circumference 7 (8, 9)" / 17.78 (20.3, 22.9) cm

MATERIALS

Brooklyn Tweed LOFT (100% Targhee-Columbia wool; 275 yds / 251 m per 50g ball)

» [MC] Fossil; 1 skein
» [CC] Cast Iron; 1 skein

1 set US #2 / 2.75 mm double-point needles

Stitch marker (optional)
Waste yarn or stitch holder
Yarn needle

GAUGE

8 sts = 1" / 2.54 cm in stranded colour work pattern

8.5 rnds = 1" / 2.54 cm in stranded colourwork pattern

PATTERN

Cuff

Using MC, CO 56 (64, 76) sts using the Long-tail cast on, or any other stretchy cast on. Distribute sts evenly across 4 needles—14 (16, 19) sts on each. The needles will now be known as N1, 2, 3 and 4 respectively. Being careful not to twist sts, prepare to work in the rnd working the cuff as follows:

Rnd 1: [K2tbl, p2], repeat across all sts.

Repeat Rnd 1 for the next 7 (9, 11) rnds, for a total of 8 (10, 12) rnds of ribbing.

Small and Medium sizes only:
Work 1 rnd in St st.

Large size only:
Work 1 rnd in St st increasing 1 st at beginning of N1 and N3 - 78 sts.

Mitten Body

Work from chart S, M or L, following from right to left.

Please note that the chart shows every st in every rnd.

Continue working from the chart until Rnd 24 (29, 31) where there is a mark denoting thumb placement.

THUMB PLACEMENT

For LH mitten: Work across all sts on N 1, 2 and 3. Work the first 2 (3, 5) sts on N4. Using a 15"/38 cm piece of waste yarn knit the next 9 (10, 11) sts on N4. Slip these sts back onto the LH needle and continue to work in pattern. Work the last 3 sts rem on N4 - 14 (16, 20) sts remain on N4.

For RH mitten: Work across N1 and N2. Knit the first 3 sts on N3. Using the 15"/38 cm piece of waste yarn knit the next 9 (10, 11) sts on N3. Slip these sts back onto the RH needle and continue to work in pattern.

Work the remaining sts on N3 – 14 (16, 19) sts rem on N3. Work across all sts on N4 in pattern.

If making fingerless mittens, please work from the following directions. If making regular mittens please skip the following directions and proceed to the Mitten Body (continued) section.

FINGERLESS MITTENS

Work to the end of Rnd 36, or until mitten reaches just below the recipient's knuckles, or desired length.

Small and medium sizes only:

Working with MC only work the next 2 rnds in St st.

Complete fingerless mitten body as follows:

Large size only:

Working with MC only, decrease 1 st at the beginning of N1 and N3 on next rnd – 76 sts.

All sizes:

Rnd 1: Knit.

Rnds 2 – 6: Using MC only, work [k2tbl, p2] rib across all sts.

Bind off all sts loosely.

FINGERLESS MITTEN THUMB

Pick up 9 (10, 11) sts both above and below the sts held on the waste yarn, along with 4 total sts from each end of the thumb hole or a total of 22 (24, 26) sts. sts, discarding the waste yarn when finished.

Divide the sts thus:

- » Small: N1 – 5 sts, N2 – 6 sts, N3 – 5 sts, N4 – 6 sts
- » Medium: 6 sts on each needle
- » Large: N1 – 6 sts, N2 – 7 sts, N3 – 6 sts, N4 – 7 sts

Work the thumb, starting from the outer lower corner and working across the front of the thumb.

Work the thumb as follows:

Rnd 1: With MC, k all sts.

Continue working Rnd 1 until thumb reaches just below the recipient's thumb joint, or desired length, working to the end of N4. Complete the thumb as follows:

Small and Large sizes only:

Decrease 1 st from N2 and 4 on last rnd – 20 (24) sts.

All sizes:

Rnds 1–4: Work [k2tbl, p2] rib across all sts.

Bind off all sts loosely. Proceed to Finishing directions below.

Mitten Body (continued)

Continue working from the appropriate chart until Rnd 57 (63, 75) where the finger decreases begin.

FINGER DECREASES

The finger decreases can be successfully executed working only from the chart or from the instructions below (or both.)

The finger decreases are worked with MC only. Decrease for the fingertips as follows:

- » N1: Slip the first st, k1, psso, work across all remaining sts in pattern.
- » N2: Work across all sts in pattern until 2 sts remain, k2tog.
- » N3: Slip the first sts, k1, psso, work across all remaining sts in pattern.
- » N4: Work across all sts in pattern until 2 sts remain, k2tog.

Repeat this until 20 (20, 30) sts remain, working the final rnd to the end of N4. Slip all sts from N2 onto N1, and all sts from N4 onto N3 – 10 (10, 15) sts on each needle. Break yarn, leaving a generous amount to graft remaining sts. Kitchener Stitch the top of the mitten closed.

Thumb

Pick up 9 (10, 11) sts both above and below the sts held on the waste yarn, along with 4 total sts from each end of the thumb hole or a total of 22 (24, 26) sts. sts, discarding the waste yarn when finished.

Divide the sts thus:

- » Small size: N1 – 5 sts, N2 – 6 sts, N3 – 5 sts, N4 – 6 sts
- » Medium size: 6 sts on each needle
- » Large size: N1 – 6 sts, N2 – 7 sts, N3 – 6 sts, N4 – 7 sts

Begin working thumb, starting from the outer lower corner and working across the front of the thumb.

Rnd 1: With MC, knit all sts.

Continue working Rnd 1 until thumb reaches to about the tip of the recipient's thumb, or desired length, working to the end of N4. Work thumb decreases as follows:

» N1: Slip 1 st, k1, psso, work all remaining sts in pattern.

» N2: Work all sts in pattern until 2 sts remain, k2tog.

» N3: Slip 1 sts, k1, psso, work all remaining st in pattern.

» N4: Work all sts in pattern until 2 sts remain, k2tog.

Repeat until 10 (8, 10) sts remain. Break yarn, leaving a generous amount to close up top of mitten. Draw yarn tail through remaining sts several times to close top of thumb.

Finishing

Weave in ends. Place mitten beneath a damp tea towel and press with a hot iron set to the wool setting to steam block.

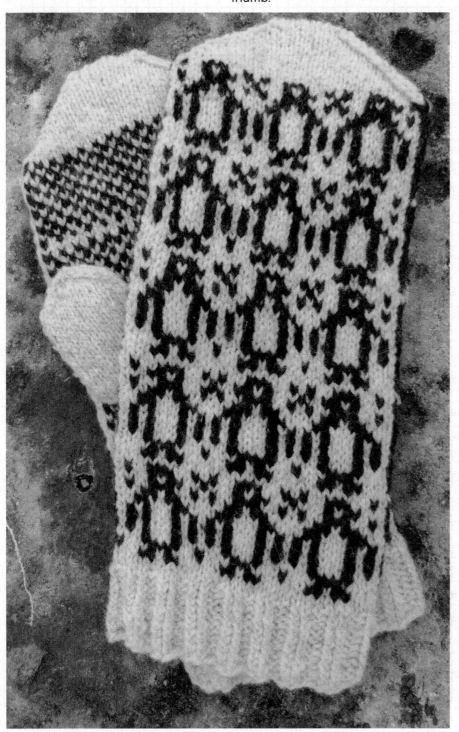

☐ Knit MC

■ Knit CC

☑ K2tog

◩ Slip 1, k1, psso

☐ Right thumb placement

☐ Left thumb placement

☐ No stitch

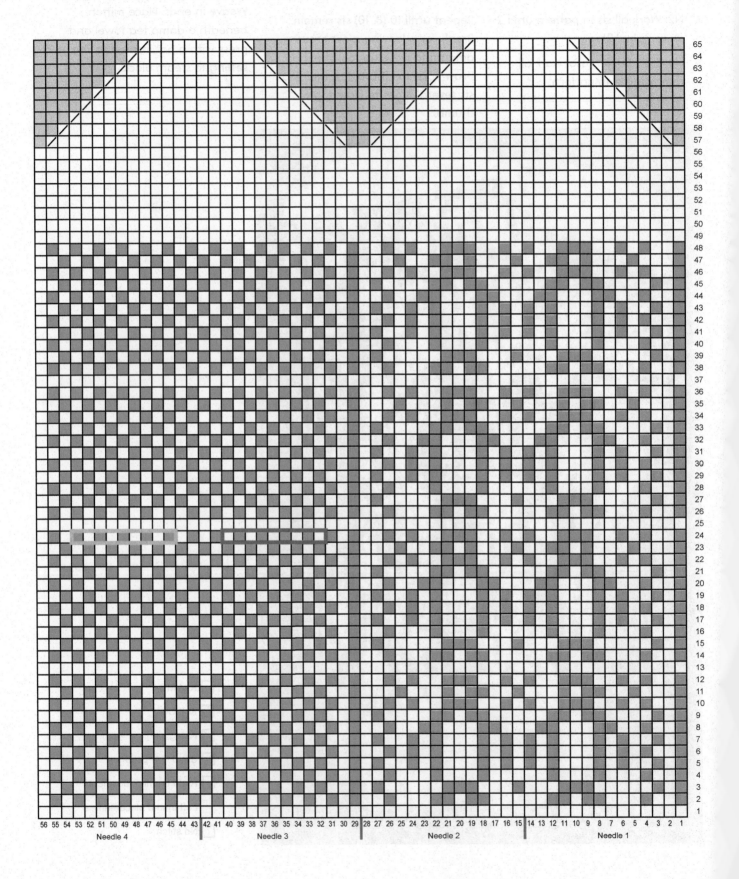

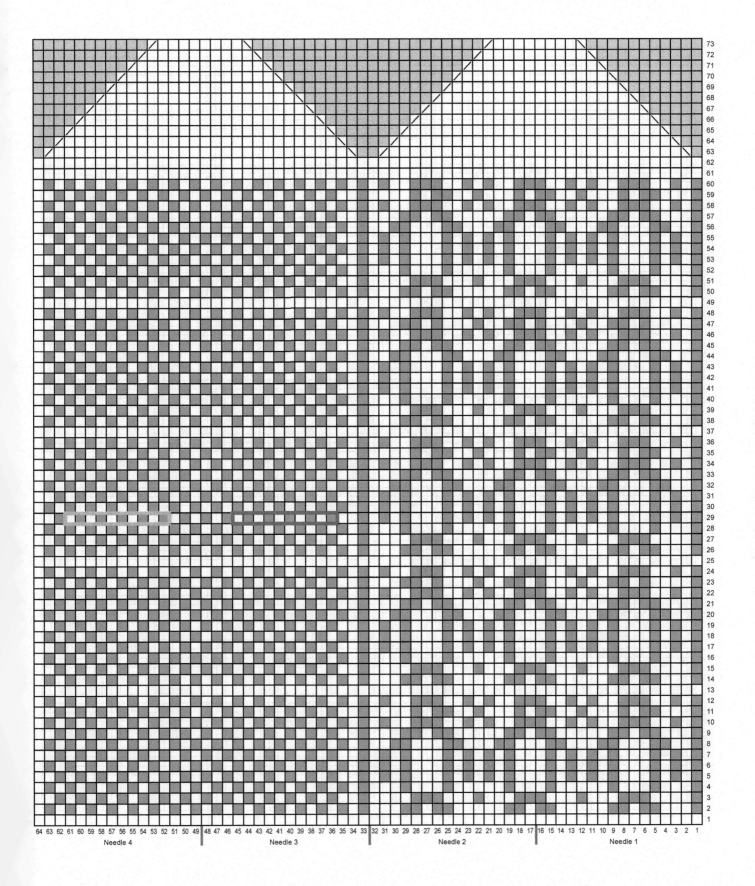

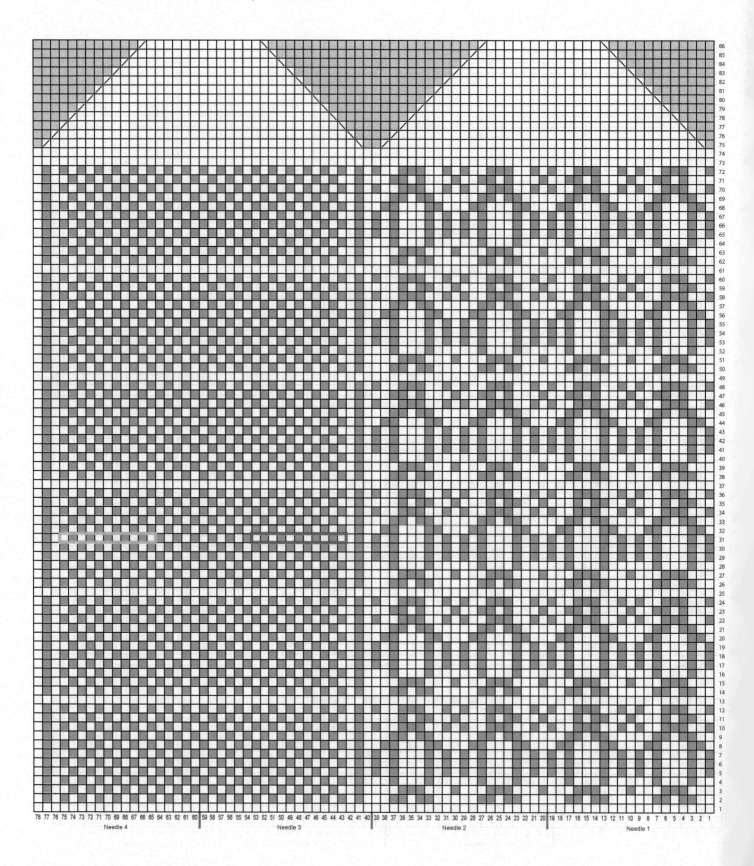

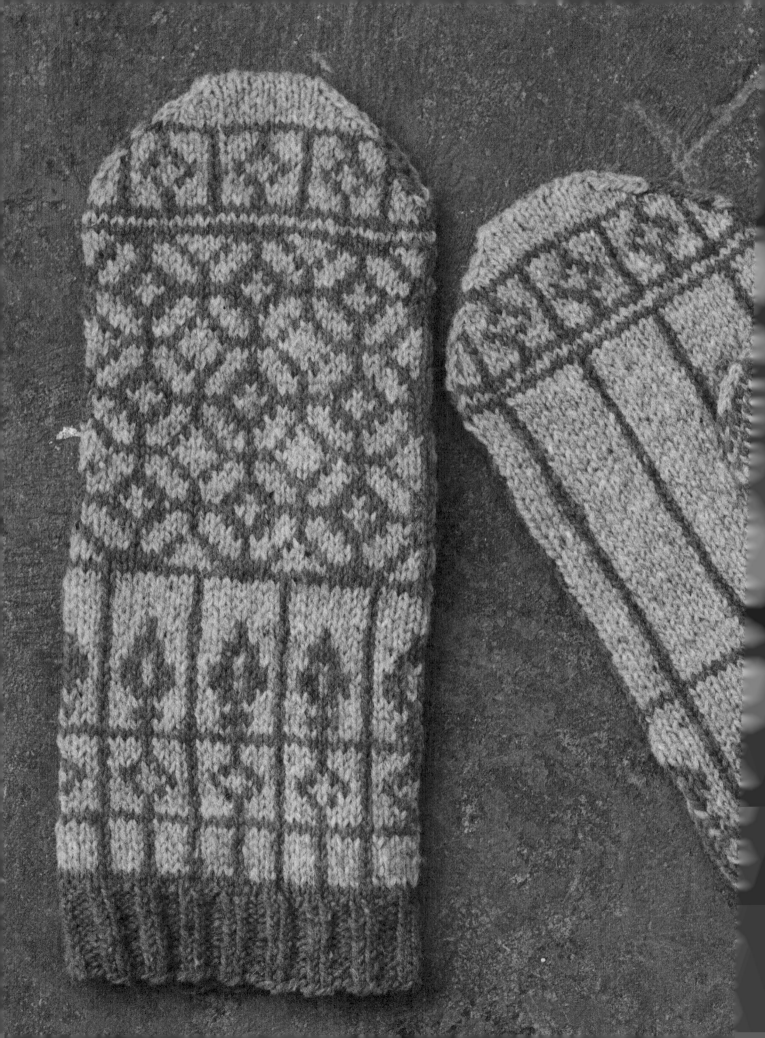

I spent New Year's Day 2012 wandering around the magnificent Abney Park, a Victorian cemetery in north London. It was a mild January day; the trees were still bare but there was plenty of green about. A particular highlight was the abandoned Neo-Gothic chapel in the centre of the park. Now in ruins, its gratings and gates inspired these mittens. I just had to make them in shades of green but they would look equally lovely knitted in shades of brick, iron and rust.

SIZES

Women's M (L); shown in size M

FINISHED MEASUREMENTS

Length 10.25"/26.03 cm

Palm Circumference 8 (9)"/20.3 (22.9) cm

MATERIALS

Brooklyn Tweed LOFT (100% Targhee-Columbia wool; 275 yds / 251 m per 50g skein)

» [MC] Tent; 1 skein
» [CC] Foothills; 1 skein

1 set US #2 / 2.75 mm double-point needles

Stitch marker (optional)
Waste yarn or stitch holder
Yarn needle

GAUGE

8 sts = 1" / 2.54 cm in stranded colour work pattern

7.5 rnds = 1" / 2.54 cm in stranded colourwork pattern

PATTERN

Cuff

Using the MC, CO 64 (72) sts using the Long-tailcast on, or any other stretchy cast on. Distribute sts evenly across 4 needles—16 (18) sts on each. The needles will now be known as N1, 2, 3 and 4 respectively. Being careful not to twist sts, Begin to work in the round, working the cuff as follows:

Rnd 1: [K2tbl, p2] repeat across all sts.

Repeat Rnd 1 for the next 9 (11) rnds, for a total of 10 (12) rnds of ribbing. Ribbing is complete. Work all sts of the next rnd in St st.

MITTEN BODY

Work from chart M or L, following from left to right.

Please note that the charts show every st in every rnd.

Continue working from the chosen chart until Rnd 29 where there is a mark denoting thumb placement.

THUMB PLACEMENT

For LH mitten: Work across all sts on N1, 2 and 3. Work the first 3 (4) sts on N4. Using a 15"/38 cm piece of waste yarn knit the next 10 (11) sts on N4. Slip these sts back onto the LH needle and continue to work in pattern. Work the last 3 sts rem on N4 - 16 (18) sts remain on N4.

For RH mitten: Work across N1 and N2. Knit the first 3 sts on N3. Using the 15"/38 cm piece of waste yarn knit the next 10 sts on N3. Slip these sts back onto the RH needle and continue to work in pattern. Work the last 3 sts on N3 - 16 (18) sts rem on N3. Work across all sts on N4 in pattern.

If making fingerless mittens, please work from the following directions. If making regular mittens please skip the following directions and proceed to the Mitten Body (continued) section.

FINGERLESS MITTENS

Work to the end of Rnd 40 or until mitten reaches just below the recipient's knuckles, or desired length. Working with MC only work the next 2 rnds in St st. Complete fingerless mitten body as follows:

Rnds 3–7: Work [k2tbl, p2] rib across all sts.

Bind off all sts loosely.

FINGERLESS MITTEN THUMB

Pick up 10 (11) sts both above and below the sts held on the waste yarn, along with a total of 4 sts from either side of the thumb-hole for a total of 24 (26) sts.

Medium: Divide the sts evenly across 4 needles, so you have 6 sts on each needle.

» Large: Divide the sts across 4 needles thus: N1 - 6 sts, N2 - 7 sts, N3 - 6 sts, N4 - 7 sts.

Work the thumb, starting from the outer lower corner and working across the front of the thumb. This first needle will be known as N1, with the other needles known as N2, N3 and N4 respectively. Work the thumb as follows:

Rnd 1: [K1 MC, k1 CC] repeat across all sts.
Rnd 2: [K1 CC, k1 MC] repeat across all sts.

Continue working Rnds 1 and 2 until thumb reaches just below the recipient's thumb joint, or desired length, working to the end of N4.

Complete thumb as follows:

Large size only:

Decrease 1 st on N2 and N4 - 24 sts.

All sizes:

Rnds 1–4: Using MC only, work [k2tbl, p2] rib across all sts.

Bind off all sts loosely.

Mitten Body (continued)

Continue working from your chart until Rnd 67 (75), where the finger decreases begin.

FINGER DECREASES

The finger decreases can be successfully executed working only from your chart or from the instructions below (or both.)

» N1: Slip the first st, k1, psso, work across all remaining sts in pattern.

» N2: Work across all sts in pattern until 2 sts remain, k2tog.

» N3: Slip the first st, k1, psso, work across all remaining sts in pattern.

» N4: Work across all sts in pattern until 2 sts remain, k2tog.

Repeat until 20 sts remain, working the final rnd to the end of N4. There should now be 5 sts on each needle. Slip all sts from N2 onto N1, and all sts from N4 onto N3 - 10 sts on each needle. Break yarn, leaving a generous amount to graft remaining sts. Kitchener Stitch the top of the mitten closed. Prepare to work thumb.

Thumb

Pick up 10 (11) sts both above and below the sts held on the waste yarn, along with a total of 4 sts from either side of the thumb-hole for a total of 24 (26) sts.

Medium: Divide the sts evenly across 4 needles, so you have 6 sts on each needle.

» Large: Divide the sts across 4 needles thus: N1- 6 sts, N2 - 7 sts, N3 - 6 sts, N4 - 7 sts.

Begin working thumb, starting from the outer lower corner and working across the front of the thumb. The needles will be known as N1, 2, 3 and 4 respectively.

Rnd 1: [K1 MC, k1 CC] repeat across all sts.
Rnd 2: [K1 CC, k1 MC] repeat across all sts.

Continue working rnds 1 and 2 until thumb reaches to about the tip of the recipient's thumb or desired length, working to the end of N4.

Work thumb decreases as follows:

- » N1: Slip 1 st, k1, psso, work all remaining sts in pattern.
- » N2: Work all sts in pattern until 2 sts remain, k2tog.
- » N3: Slip 1 st, k1, psso, work all remaining stitches in pattern.

- » N4: Work all sts in pattern until 2 sts remain, k2tog.

Repeat until 8 (10) sts remain. Break yarn, leaving a generous amount to close up top of mitten. Draw yarn tail through 8 (10) remaining sts several times to close top of thumb.

Finishing

Weave in ends. Place mitten beneath a damp tea towel and press with a hot iron set to the wool setting to steam block.

- ☐ Knit MC
- ▦ Knit CC
- ▨ K2tog
- ◩ Slip 1, k1, psso
- ☐ Right thumb placement
- ☐ Left thumb placement
- ▦ No stitch

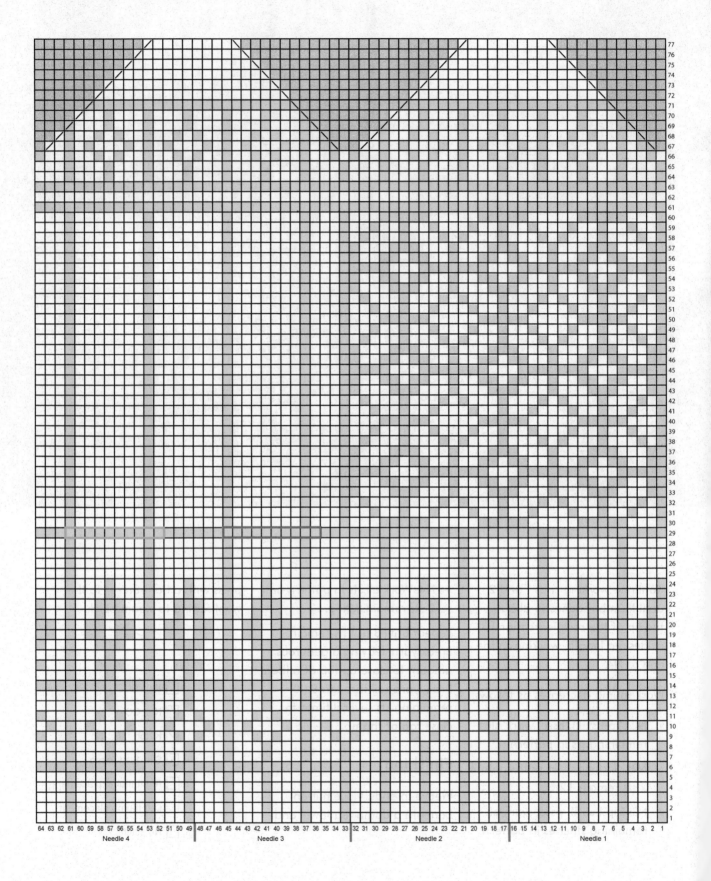

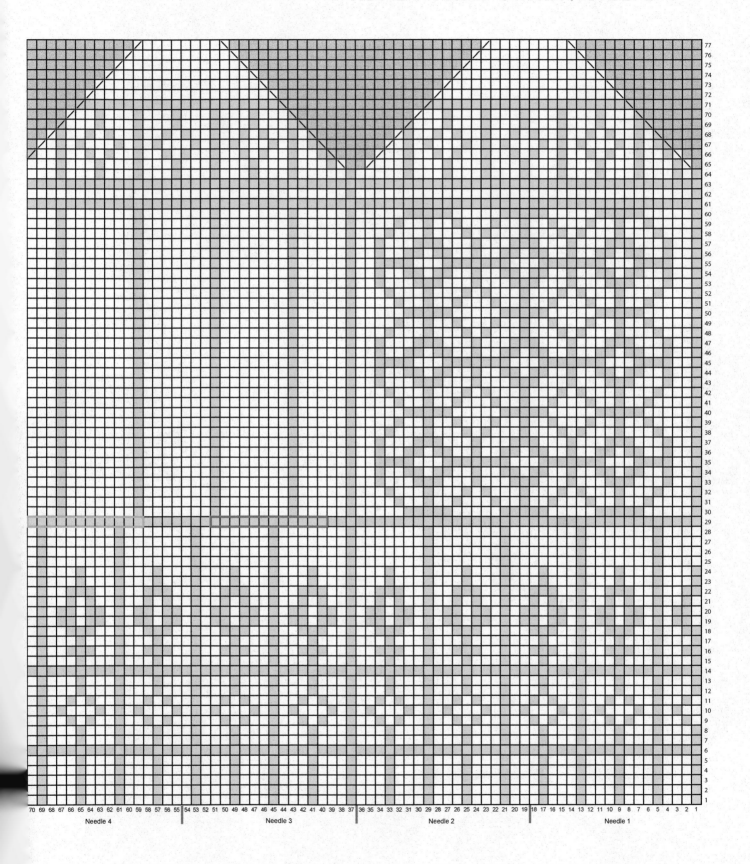

WHEATFIELD

WHEAT FIELDS ARE A CONSTANT COMPANION ON ROAD TRIPS IN Southwestern Ontario. Winter wheat is planted in autumn and brilliant green fields emerge when the snow recedes in earliest spring. These mittens capture a drive home on Highway 401 in high summer while farmers work into the evening to harvest the now-mature grain from dusty golden fields. Each bushel carries the memories of the changing seasons and place where it was grown.

SIZES

Women's M (L); shown in size M.

FINISHED MEASUREMENTS

Palm Circumference 8 (9)" / 20.32 (22.86) cm

Length 9.5 (10.95)" / 24.1 (27.81) cm

MATERIALS

Brooklyn Tweed LOFT (100% Targhee-Columbia wool; 275 yds / 251 m per 50 g ball)

» [MC] Pumpernickel; 1 skein
» [CC] Hayloft; 1 skein

1 set US #2/2.75 mm double-point needles

Stitch marker (optional)
Waste yarn or stitch holder
Yarn needle

GAUGE

8 sts = 1"/2.54 cm in stranded colour work pattern

8.25 rnds = 1"/2.54 cm in stranded colourwork pattern

PATTERN

Cuff

Using the MC, CO 64 (72) sts using the Long-tail cast on, or any other stretchy cast on.

Distribute sts evenly across 4 needles—16 (18) sts on each. The needles will now be known as N1, 2, 3 and 4 respectively. Being careful not to twist sts, begin to work in the rnd working the cuff as follows:

Rnd 1: [K2tbl, p2] repeat across all sts.

Repeat Rnd 1 for the next 9 (11) rnds, for a total of 10 (12) rnds of ribbing. Work all sts of the next rnd in St st. Prepare to work body of mitten, working from chart M or L.

Mitten Body

Work from your chart, following from right to left.

Please note that the chart shows every st in every rnd.

Continue working from your chart until Rnd 30 (32), where there is a mark denoting thumb placement.

THUMB PLACEMENT

For LH mitten: Work across all sts on N 1, 2, and 3, then work the first 3 (4) sts on N4. Using a 15"/38 cm piece of waste yarn k the next 10 (11) sts on N4. Slip these sts back onto the LH needle and continue to work in pattern. Work the last 3 sts remaining on N4 - 16 (18) sts remain on N4.

For RH mitten: Work across N1 and N2. Knit the first 3 sts on N3. Using the 15"/38 cm piece of waste yarn knit the next 10 (11) sts on N3. Slip these sts back onto the RH needle and continue to work in pattern, to the end of the needle - 16 (18) sts remain on N3. Work across all sts on N4 in pattern.

If making fingerless mittens please work from the following directions. If making regular mittens please skip the following directions and proceed to the Mitten Body (continued) section.

FINGERLESS MITTENS

Work to the end of Rnd 38, or until mitten reaches just below the recipient's knuckles (or desired length.) Working with MC only work the next 2 rnds in St st. Prepare to complete fingerless mitten body as follows:

Rnds 3–7: Work [k2tbl, p2] rib across all sts.

Bind off all sts loosely.

FINGERLESS MITTEN THUMB

Pick up 10 (11) sts both above and below the sts held on the waste yarn, along with 4 total sts from either side of the thumb hole, for a total of 24 (26) sts, discarding the waste yarn when finished. Divide the sts across your 4 needles as follows:

» Medium: 6 sts on each needle

» Large: N1 and 3: 6 sts, N2 and 4: 7 sts.

Prepare to work thumb, starting from the outer lower corner and working across the front of the thumb. This first needle will be known as N1, with the other needles known as N2, N3 and N4 respectively. Work the thumb as follows:

Rnd 1: With MC, knit all stitches.

Continue working Rnd 1 until thumb reaches just below the recipient's thumb joint (or desired length,) working to the end of N4.

Large size only:

Decrease one st on N2 and 4 - 24 sts.

All sizes:

Rnds 1–4: Using MC only, work k2tbl, p2 rib across all sts.

Bind off all sts loosely.

Proceed to Finishing directions below.

Mitten Body (continued)

Continue working from your chart until Rnd 61 (72) where the finger decreases begin.

The finger decreases can be successfully executed working only from your chart or from the instructions below (or both.)

The finger decreases are worked with MC only. Decrease for the fingertips as follows:

» N1: Slip the first st, k1, psso, work across all remaining sts in pattern.

» N2: Work across all sts in pattern until 2 stitches remain, k2tog.

» N3: Slip the first sts, k1, psso, work across all remaining sts in pattern.

» N4: Work across all sts in pattern until 2 sts remain, k2tog.

Repeat this until 24 sts remain, working the final rnd to the end of N4. There should now be 6 sts on each needle Slip all sts from N2 onto N1, and all sts from N4 onto N3 - 12 sts on each needle. Break yarn, leaving a generous amount to graft remaining sts. Kitchener Stitch the top of the mitten closed.

Thumb

Pick up 10 (11) sts both above and below the sts held on the waste yarn, along with 4 total sts from either side of the thumb hole for a total of 24 (26) sts, discarding the waste yarn when finished. Divide the sts across your 4 needles as follows:

» Medium: 6 sts on each needle

» Large: N1 and 3: 6 sts, N2 and 4: 7 sts

Begin working thumb, starting from the outer lower corner and working across the front of the thumb.

Work the thumb as follows:

Rnd 1: With MC, knit all sts.

Continue working Rnd 1 until thumb reaches to about the tip of the recipient's thumb (or desired length,) working to the end of N4.

- » N1: Slip 1 st, k1, psso, work all remaining sts in pattern.

- » N2: Work all sts in pattern until 2 sts remain, k2tog.

- » N3: Slip 1 st, k1, psso, work all remaining sts in pattern.

- » N4: Work all sts in pattern until 2 sts remain, k2tog.

Repeat until 8 (10) sts remain. Break yarn, leaving a generous amount to close up top of mitten. Draw yarn tail through 8 remaining sts several times to close top of thumb.

Finishing

Weave in ends. Place mitten beneath a damp tea towel and press with a hot iron set to the wool setting to steam block.

☐ Knit Main Colour

☐ Knit Contrast Colour

☑ K2tog

◻ Slip 1, k1, psso

☐ Right thumb placement

☐ Left thumb placement

☐ No stitch

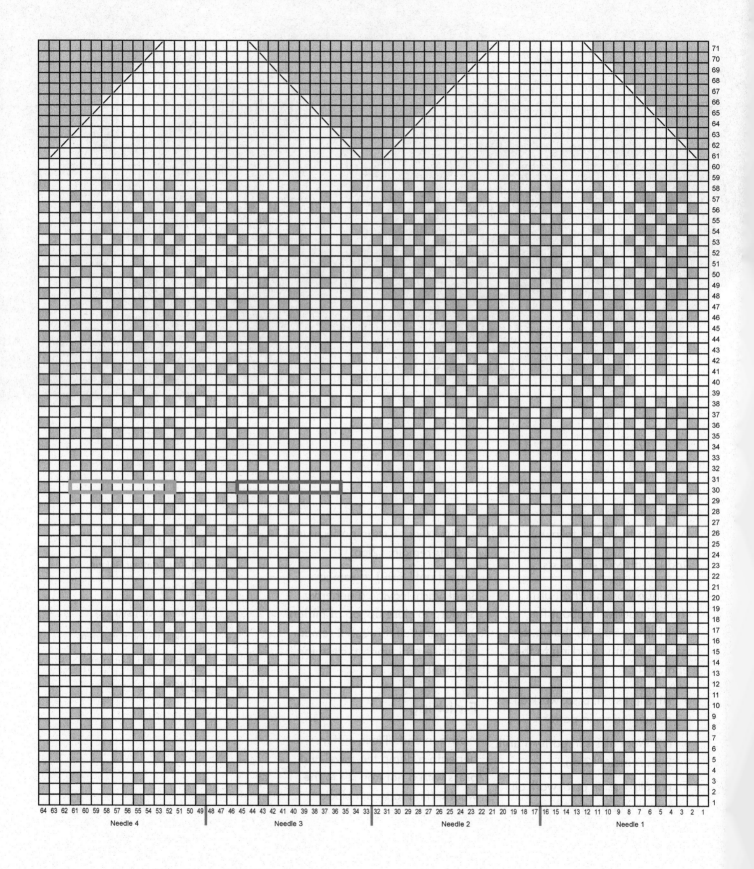

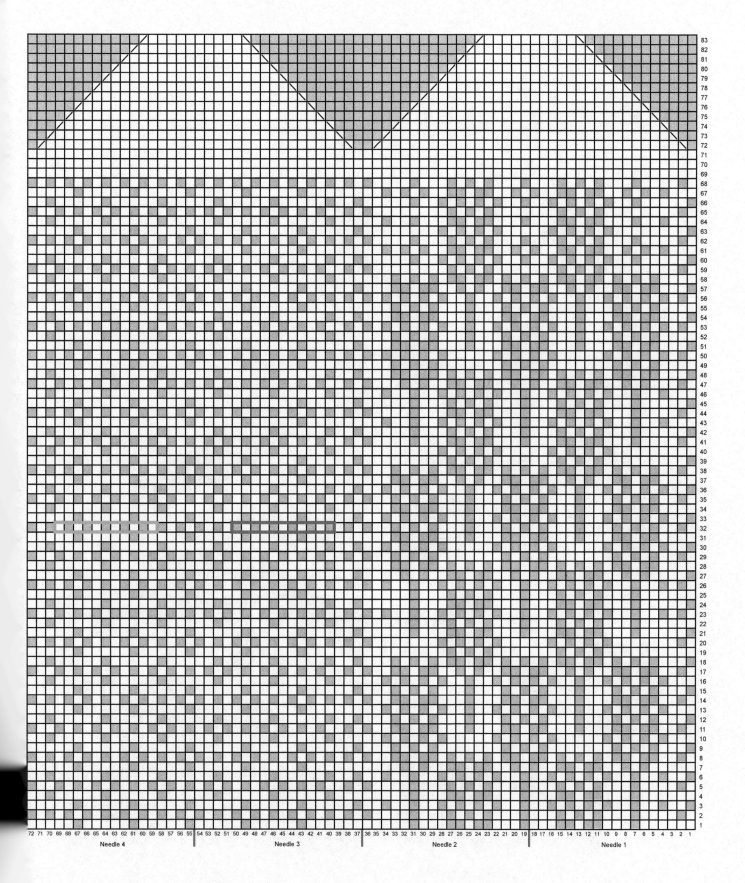

A note on the type

The text of this book is set in Toronto Subway, a font based on the signage lettering of Toronto's original subway stations. Its straight lines and overall elegance are indicative of the mid-century modern style popular when the subway first opened in 1954.

The original unnamed font was abandoned by the Toronto Transit Commission sometime in the seventies and is rarely found in later additions to the system. Examples of the original lettering can still be seen in the station identification signs of older stations.

David Vereschagin of Quadrat Communications developed Toronto Subway from rubbings he made of station identifications and photographs of original signage. His quasi-archaeological efforts have preserved a unique part of Toronto's urban aesthetic character.

A note about the author

(Spilly) Jane Dupuis has independently published over a hundred knitting patterns, and her work has appeared in numerous print and electronic publications. This is her first book. You can keep up with her latest patterns and musings on her blog at http://spillyjane.blogspot.com. Jane lives in Windsor, Ontario with her husband and their avian companion, Earl, the African Grey parrot.

Acknowledgments

There are numerous people, besides myself, without whom this book would not exist. In no particular order I would like to thank my mom, who introduced me to knitting as a child; every friend and acquaintance who asked "Why don't you have a book?"; Shannon Okey at CP who asked "Why don't you write a book?" and provided the framework to make it happen; Andi Smith, who spent hours tech editing the charts and styling the photographs for the tutorials; and Kate Davies for writing a wonderful forward.

Thank you to Jared Flood and everyone and Brooklyn Tweed, and Stacey Winklepleck and all at Knit Picks for generously providing the necessary yarn and supplies to knit all the sample mittens.

Last, but not least, thanks to my husband, David, for assistance with editing, photography, overall moral support, and limitless patience.

ABOUT COOPERATIVE PRESS

Cooperative Press (formerly anezka media) was founded in 2007 by Shannon Okey, a voracious reader as well as writer and editor, who had been doing freelance acquisitions work, introducing authors with projects she believed in to editors at various publishers.

Although working with traditional publishers can be very rewarding, there are some books that fly under their radar. They're too avant-garde, or the marketing department doesn't know how to sell them, or they don't think they'll sell 50,000 copies in a year.

5,000 or 50,000. Does the book matter to that 5,000? Then it should be published.

In 2009, Cooperative Press (cooperativepress.com) changed its named to reflect the relationships we have developed with authors working on books. We work together to put out the best quality books we can and share in the proceeds accordingly.

Thank you for supporting independent publishers and authors.

ABBREVIATIONS

» CO = cast on

» CC = contrast colour

» K = knit

» LH = left hand

» MC = main colour

» N = needle

» P = purl

» RH = right hand

» rnd / rnds = round / rounds

» St st = Stockinette stitch

» st / sts = stitch / stitches

» tbl = through (the) back (of the) loop

APPENDIX

Try your hand at designing your own colourwork mittens. Just find your own pattern inspiration and translate it into stitch format using the following blank charts. Inspiration is everywhere once you start looking for it.

Included here are charts for each of the three different sizes used throughout the book in two different gauge options, both 8 and 9 stitches to the inch.

Thumb options are included for both the peasant and gusset styles. You can design your own pattern using the blank peasant or gusset charts. But if you go with the gusset thumb, remember that you will be knitting the thumb as you knit the rest of the mitten. The simple and ready-to-go lice stitch and striped gusset thumb charts will work well with any mitten design you come up with.

▣ No stitch

✱ Denotes gusset thumb placement

☐ Knit MC

▧ Knit CC

Ⓜ️L Make 1 left

Ⓜ️R Make 1 right

— Small size

— Medium size

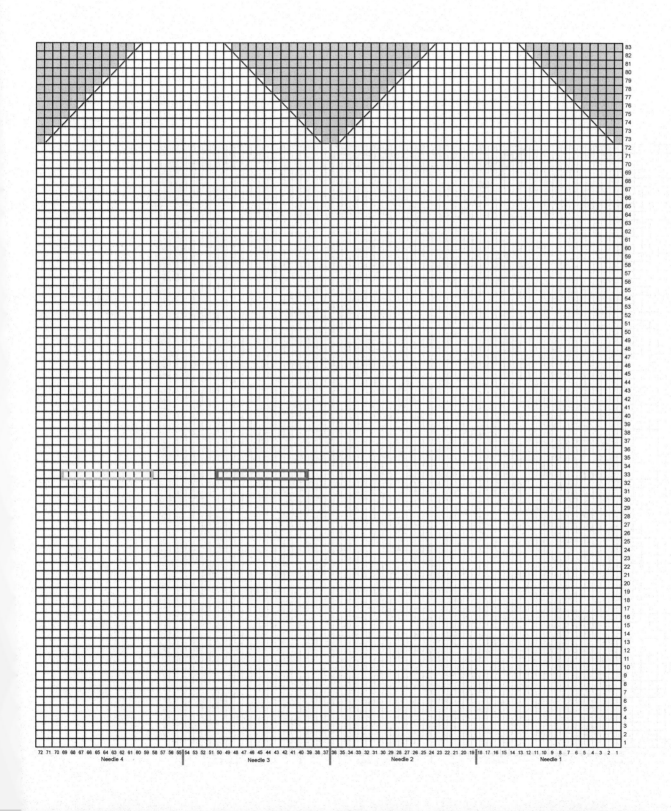

Needle 4   Needle 3   Needle 2   Needle 1

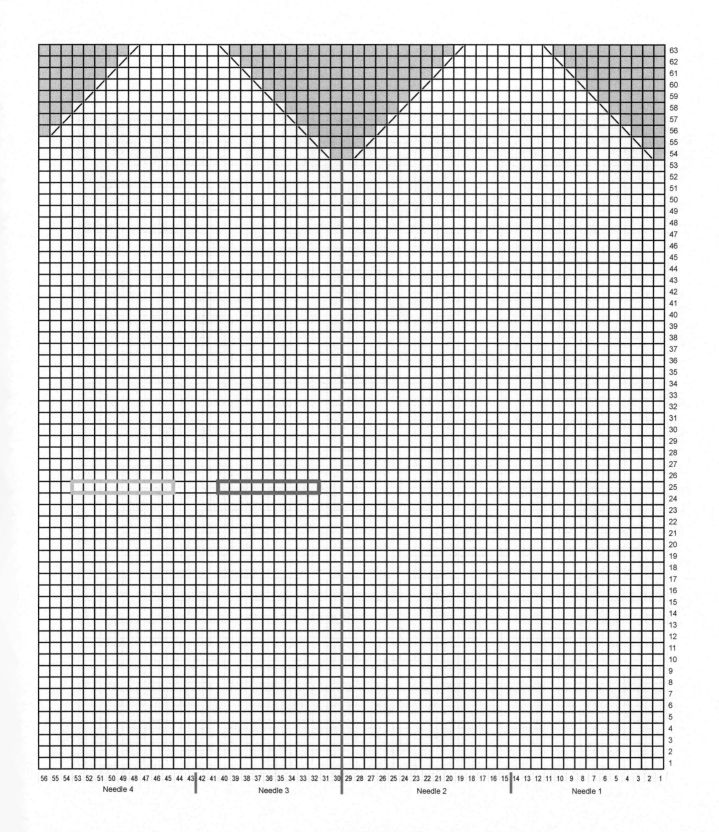

Needle 4   Needle 3   Needle 2   Needle 1

Needle 4   Needle 3   Needle 2   Needle 1

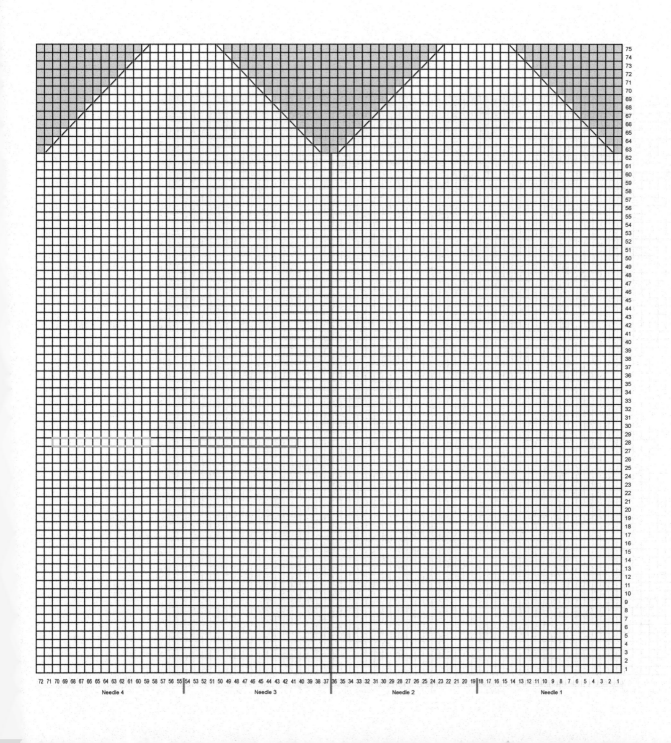

9 STITCHES TO THE INCH, SMALL

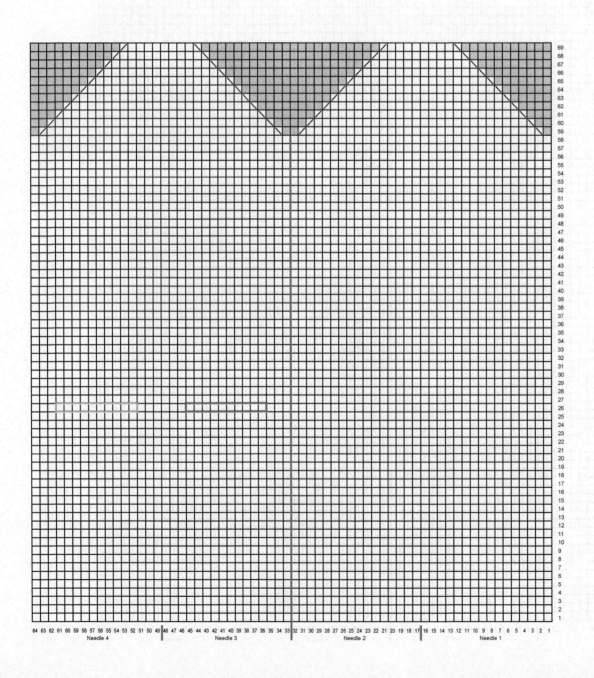

GUSSET THUMB, PLAIN (3 SIZES)

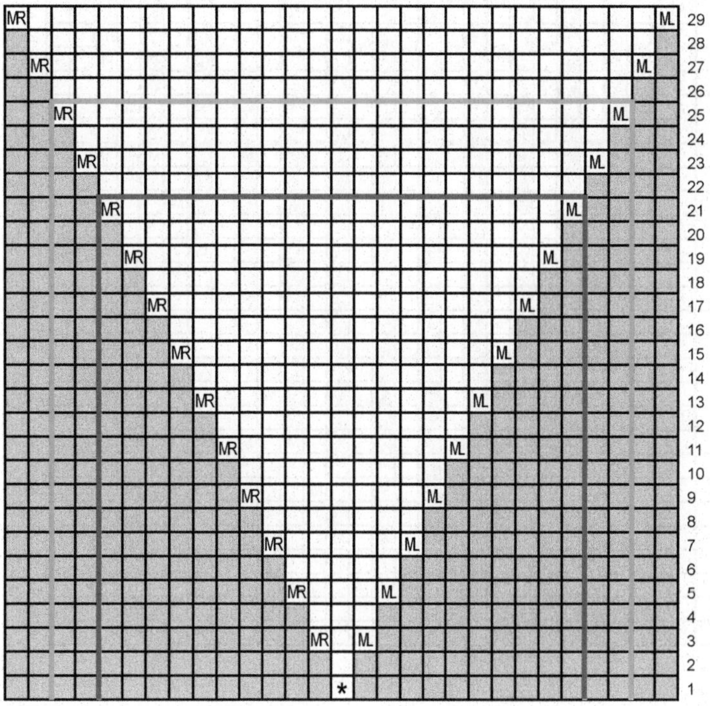

GUSSET THUMB, STRIPED (3 SIZES)

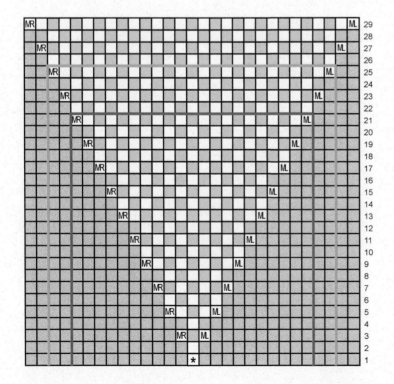

□ Main Colour
▨ Contrast Colour

GUSSET THUMB, LICE (3 SIZES)

□ Main Colour
▨ Contrast Colour

CPSIA information can be obtained
at www.ICGtesting.com
Printed in the USA
LVOW01s0034190316

479370LV00003B/3/P

9 781937 51368